Faith Guided Leadership

Are you the leader that
God wants you to be?

Thomas A. Mayberry

Copyright © 2011 by Thomas A. Mayberry

ISBN-10: 1463656750
ISBN-13: 978-1463656751

All rights reserved. No part of this book may be reproduced or transmitted in any form or any means, electronic or mechanical, including photocopying, recording, or by any information storage or retrieval system – except for brief quotations in critical reviews or articles, without written permission from the copyright owner.

The stories depicted in this book are a reflection of the people involved at that time and how they reacted to specific situations. This is not necessarily a representation of their overall leadership ability. Their actions do not necessarily represent the views and policies of their employers.

DEDICATION

To my wife, Cindy, whom I have been blessed with 23 years of marriage.

To my sons, Kody and Hunter. I pray that you never lose touch of what is truly important in life.

Contents

Acknowledgments	i
Introduction	1
Chapter One: Managing or Leading	11
Chapter Two Qualities of a Strong Leader	23
Chapter Three What Defines Your Leadership Style	59
Chapter Four How does having God in the center of your life influence your style?	75
Chapter Five Creating a Stress Free Work Environment	91
Chapter Six Getting the Best out of Your Team	113
Chapter Seven Reward, Recognition and Respect	125

Chapter Eight
    Respect – The Starting Point   137

Chapter Nine
    It Starts with You   143

Chapter Ten
    Stay Grounded in Your Faith   149

Application in Your Life   157

ACKNOWLEDGMENTS

Thank you to my administrative staff for being an inspiration to me to become a better leader. You have shown how well a team can perform when they all work toward the same vision. I am so proud of you.

Thank you to my co-workers for putting up with my continual question lately, "What do you think about this for my book?" and for giving me feedback and confidence.

Thank you to Stephanie Keller for hours of editing work for the book.

Thank you to my parents for "raising me right." You have seen my struggles in life, but you have always supported me with unconditional love. It means a lot.

Introduction

It was December 1981 and I was ready to take on the business world. I received my bachelor's degree in business management and was ready for my first challenge. I was broke, but owed little in student loans. The grocery store that I worked at since I was 16 needed an assistant manager. I was offered the position and took it. I soon learned that in a small town with a privately owned store, there would be no room for advancement. I had much bigger plans. I moved back to the college town, where I went to school, and looked for another job. I got into the pizza business and started chasing that corporate carrot. It did not matter what I needed to do. I was determined to excel in the business world. I was going to move up the corporate ladder rapidly. If my supervisor wanted me to move to another state to get ahead, I did. I had completed the six month training program. I started as a manager in training for $3.45 per hour. That was 10¢ more than minimum wage. So after six months, I was extremely eager to manage my first store. The area supervisor stopped by the store on a Tuesday and I reminded him that I was trained and ready for a promotion. I was living in Colorado at the time. He asked me what I thought about Kansas. I told him that Kansas was not a bad state. He asked me if I would be interested in running a store in Leavenworth, Kansas. I definitely was interested. He replied that I needed to pack my bags because they needed me to start that weekend. The way to get promoted with that company was to excel in the store that you were in and get transferred to a higher volume store. A manager got a percentage of the profits of the store as a bonus. That was a huge incentive to push harder. Many times, this involved moving with little notice. It was not unusual to get the call on Tuesday night and have to be in the new city ready to start work by Saturday night. This included the time to pack boxes, load the rental truck, drive to another state, find a place to live and unload. Needless to say, there were many boxes that moved around with me and never got unpacked.

This became my definition of success. I did not worry about what lives were affected along the way. I married in the fall of 1982. My wife, at the time, was trying to start her career path after graduating from college. When I got the call about my first promotion from being a manager in training to running my first store, I was excited and ready to move. The move was from Colorado to Kansas and I had less than a week to move my things and get started in the new position. I do not remember asking her what her thoughts were about moving. Actually, I do not think that I cared. I just assumed that she would be a "good wife" and move with her husband. That was my first real lesson in marriage. I failed that lesson. Three moves later including a move to two different cities in Texas, I had failed more times. I still did not learn after we divorced in 1985. I was hard nosed, cut throat and did not care much about who I possibly hurt along the way to get to the top. I had turnover problems with my staff since I did not tolerate poor performance out of anyone. I had no patience. I was not forgiving. There was no such thing as a second chance. I was determined to be the best manager that I could. I would read a lot of management books and observed the way my supervisors managed me. I attended many seminars, read books on anything related to managing people and kept trying to picture myself up in front of a group and teaching people how to be better leaders. Remember, I was going to be the best. I eventually became a certified trainer of all of the corporate management classes. I had a vision/goal in my late 20's to write a book and be a motivational speaker. I felt that my management style was successful and others could benefit from my talents. I was arrogant at the time. I was like a troubleshooter for the company. I could take over a problem account and in a short amount of time I would have it running smoothly and making the profits that my supervisors expected out of it. I finally got tired of transferring from one store to another and fixing it. I wanted to be promoted to area supervisor. It was not happening quickly enough. I would try to apply a lot of the principles that I had read about management. I have tried to copy many of the styles of the managers that I worked for. I kept asking myself "Why am I not getting promoted?"

I ended up setting up an appointment with a franchise owner with six stores in another part of Texas. I spent about an hour convincing him that it was in his best interest to have an area supervisor. It took me about an hour to convince him that I was the person to hire for the newly created position. It was in this new town that I met my second wife. As you can see, I was still on the path of career over marriage. I married Cindy in 1988 and was still chasing the dream of getting to the top of a corporation. I always put my career before my family. I justified it by telling myself that I was just being a better provider. I still had six more moves from state to state before we settled down in Tennessee. I did not take time off when my sons were born. I have major regrets from being that selfish, but I can not rewrite history. I was not a good husband and father at the time and wish I could change that. Our oldest son, Kody was born in Texas and our youngest, Hunter, was born in Michigan. I continued to change positions and move around the country, dragging my wife and kids with me. I was unaware of the level of stress I was putting on my relationship with my family at that time. It was not until I was close to losing another marriage that I realized where my priorities should be. When we moved to Tennessee and my oldest child was in kindergarten, we stopped moving. I can not thank Cindy enough for raising two small boys alone while I worked in Tennessee for 3 months before moving them here. They were still in Colorado and I was going through a 10 week training program in Nashville. I knew when I completed it I would be relocated to somewhere in a five state region. It was another selfish move on my part. She gave me a wake up call when we moved here. With her influence, I decided that there were more important things in life than work. I switched companies one more time to get a Monday through Friday, mostly day shift position. I started spending more quality time with my family. I attended baseball and football practices and games. We joined a family bowling league. We also started going to church on a regular basis. I started to see a change in my life.

The same approach showed throughout my leadership style. As the years went by, I kept that vision of writing a book and being a motivational speaker, but developed my leadership style into what it is today.

My management style has developed and changed over the years. I am no longer the aggressive manager that I was at the start of my career. The teams that I am in charge of now are so much stronger than I have ever had in the past. My approach to leadership has influenced the strength of my teams. I look back at the teams that I had in my early years of management and feel now that there probably was not much of a team in actuality. It was centered on them serving me. They were there to make me more money. They supported my goal of getting bigger bonus checks and the next promotion. I can see now that the family relationships at home were the same kind of relationships I had with my co-workers. I treated them poorly as well.

I did not realize until recently that my current style of management could be contributed to my faith in God. I have always been a religious person. I just do not think that I had given God enough credit for what has taken place in my life. I do not believe in coincidences. I think that everything happens for a purpose. God has control of my life, even when I do not realize it. I look back at my life and the different situations that I was put into. I look back at the good managers that I worked for and the bad managers. This was training that God was giving me throughout my life. My faith was developing along the way. When I started applying some of these religious principles, I started to notice a big impact on people around me.

Throughout my career, I have lived in different parts of the country. I have worked for many managers with very diverse ways of managing people. I do not believe that the way they manage people had anything to do with the area of the country that they work in. I think that it had more to do with how they were trained and the managers that they had worked for in the past. We learn from the people around us. When you are a manager, you influence so many people. You do not realize the different areas that your staff looks up to you. You are their role model. Can you say that you have been a good role model or a bad one? The way that we have been managed influences the way that we are going to manage people. If we are brought up in the strict environment, we will probably develop a strict environment for the people that work for us. If you are fortunate to have had a strong leader, which really cared for their team, as the first manager that you worked for, you saw firsthand the results from that type of leadership. Hopefully you had many years to develop under that manager. Sometime along the way, you will probably have the other type of experience. There are managers that are self centered. They run their team like a dictatorship. If you work for both types, you can compare the results of the two and see the difference in how the employees reacted.

I struggled at times to be my own type of manager in environments where my supervisor had a different approach that I believe was right. I was always struggling to fit in. I would go against my beliefs just to get ahead. After a while, I had had enough. I have left companies because my immediate supervisor's style did not fit my values in life. Most of the time, people do not leave companies because of their feelings toward the company. They typically leave companies because of their attitude toward their manager. In a couple of cases, I believed as if I was a failure because I did not get all of the promotions I wanted. Now I realize that I was the one succeeding because I did not have to compromise my standards. I now feel comfortable managing people with my philosophy and not worrying about how the rest of the management around me is treating their teams. I know that I can develop a strong team with my values. I can still have the same standards the other management have, but just with a different approach. Throughout this book I am going to talk about my approach to leadership. As you can see, I was not a good leader, in God's eyes for many years. It took me close to ruining two marriages and many job changes to figure out that God had plans for me. I will show you that you can be true to yourself and your beliefs.

The qualities of a good leader can be traced to the Bible. I have read many leadership books over the years. Until now, I did not realize that the most powerful leadership book in print was the Bible. The qualities of a strong leader are the same qualities that give us strong relationships. God has taught us everything we need to know about leading people, but we just have to listen to Him and follow His lead. We will explore these teachings along the way.

Chapter One
Managing or Leading

Being a good manager is not the same as being a good leader. A good manager can implement systems and keep control of these systems. That does not necessarily mean that they are a good leader. Typically, managers will have been hired to fill a management position that has been in place for a while. The systems have been in place at that company and there is no reason for major changes. Sure, there are some areas that they may adjust some of the operational procedures, but for the most part, they continue what the previous manager had started.

I have worked for people that knew that systems/policies were in place for years and would not even think about changing them. I would ask them if they thought that certain policies were fair when carried out. They would respond as though they did not agree with some of them but it was their job to follow the rules. Do not question what has been in place for some time. They are determined to enforce the policies no matter what. They take the "it's my way or the highway" approach. There is no thinking outside the box. The procedures are adequate and there is no discussion as to changing them. They will not question the system. Even though their own personal beliefs tell them that something is wrong, they will not stand up for it. Many companies like this type of manager. They do not stir up any trouble. They will do whatever they are told without giving it any thought. I believe that if you see something that is not fair in a system, that you should question it. I do not mean launch a major protest against the corporation. You may be pointing out a flaw in the system that the people that established the rules never thought about.

Some companies want to have "yes sir" people working for them. No matter what their supervisor wants, they say "yes sir." This person might be considered a strong manager for a corporation because of that attitude. They play the corporate politics. If you are friends with all of the management above you and do everything that they ask of you without questioning, they will promote you. When you look at it from the team's perspective though, you do not get the same opinion. The team takes the approach that they are working for their supervisor. A true leader is working for their team. They want to be there for their team and provide everything possible for their team to be successful. That is how they define being successful. The manager tends to be just the opposite. They want their team to be there for them in all situations and provide everything possible for them to be successful. You see this all the time with managers that are hard to work for. They have a lot of personnel turnover. They realize that this is just part of doing business and as long as they are making the money that is needed out of their department, they are fine with that. All they are focused on are profits. They may have a profitable department. Are they a good leader? Are they successful? Is this your definition of success or have they possibly limited their amount of success and profits because of the systems that they have in place? They may be considered a good manager. Could a strong leader, though, have even better results? Can having a strong team create even more profitability?

A good leader is someone who people will respect and follow. They trust in that person enough to go that extra mile because they feel like the leader truly cares about their well-being. The leader is going to take care of their needs. The leader will take care of their people. It can be compared to references in the Bible about shepherds watching over their flocks.

> **Ezekial 34:12 (English Standard Version)**
>
> As a shepherd seeks out his flock when he is among his sheep that have been scattered, so will I seek out my sheep, and I will rescue them from all places where they have been scattered on a day of clouds and thick darkness.

We are directed to look after our flock. We will keep them secure and together. The leader is also going to take care of them and treat them with respect.

Does this mean that a leader let's his team do whatever they want to? By no means does it mean that. The leader has to set the expected standards and uphold them, but not just with a "because I am the boss" approach. They just need to give their team everything that they need to be successful. They need to be fair in how they uphold the standards. You can be very strict and also be fair. It takes some effort and awareness on your part. To have the most success possible, you need to be strong as a leader and a manager. You need to have both of those talents. You need to be able to manage the systems and procedures. I believe that you need to add the more personal touch that a strong leader has.

Managing people tends to be focused on results. It is geared around specific goals and expectations. Many times the manager takes the "I am the boss, that's why" approach. Managing is taking certain processes and procedures in your business and enforcing them. Typically it is procedures that higher management has dictated. Your team has no say in what they do. Everything is already mapped out for them. They might have great ideas on how to improve the business, but are never asked. I look at managing as being somewhat one sided. The manager is always giving instruction. They're always directing traffic. One of their main tasks is to keep order in the business. Leadership is more of a two way street. You are still in charge but interacting with the team and getting their input. The team has a say in the way that they achieve the desired end result.

Most good managers are task oriented. They know what needs to be done and they are going to insure that it gets done. Sometime they are very hands off when it comes to their group and what needs to be accomplished. They give direction and then sit back and expect it to get done. This works pretty well if you have a strong team that has been around for awhile. Then there are the micromanagers. They are more of an autocrat and have the power to make things happen. They do not hesitate to use this power. The micromanager will leave nothing to chance. They will watch over every aspect of the job and allow very little if any input from the team. There are times and places where this is needed. There is no room for error on the part of the team and there can be no deviance from the plan. How can we take that next step and improve on our management skills to become a strong leader as well?

Leadership is people oriented and purpose driven. They become a trainer and coach. They are the cheerleader for the team. Team builder is a key to success. This leads to an enhanced team effort and quality results. You focus on the people that you are working with. They are the ones that make you successful. You need to develop them to their fullest potential. You need to develop a team and acknowledge that it is a team effort. The emphasis has to be on the team. Everyone has their role to play. Not everyone has the same talents. Everyone contributes to the team effort in their own way. While I was writing this book, I was bouncing ideas off of coworkers and the subject came up about how different people approach the same situations in their careers. The topic of where to position your staff to accomplish your goals has a major impact. You need to figure out the individual talents of the people that you work with. At that point you need to assign the tasks that are needed to be done to the best people for the job. It centers on your vision. What do I mean by your vision? Take a look at your goals from a different perspective. Take a bird's eye view of what you want to accomplish. This is what I would consider as your vision. Step back away from the team enough to see the big picture. You need to see and understand the flow of the projects. Where can they be improved? What are the stumbling blocks? It may not be that a person is wrong for the team. They just need to be repositioned to an area where they have stronger talents. I compare it to a chess game. Both players have the exact same set of game pieces. It is what they do with them that wins or loses the game. My oldest brother Mike used to whip me in chess while we were growing up. For some reason he always could position his pieces through out the game, short as they were, to beat me. He did not have any special pieces but knew how they interacted and could see into the future where he needed to move them to execute his plan. We should take that same approach as a leader. Why are we so quick to say that we do not have good talent working for us? "Why does the competition have such better people working for them?" We get too quick in wanting to turn over our staff and start fresh. We need to look at each of their individual talents and see where they can help the team succeed. In many cases, we have failed to lead them properly. We have not utilized their potential or placed them in the right position to enhance the team's performance. I have made moves with my staff that completely changed up their job description and approach to the business. Later on, they saw where I was going with the move and realized that they were much better off than on the path that they were on before. Take ownership in your team and do your best to enable them to reach their potential.

This is the area that your leadership skills must kick in. Your communication skills must step up to the next level. The interaction with your team and the feedback that they provide can take these managed systems to a greater team effort. You will need to develop a long term goal. This is your vision for the future. I always have believed that the further you are up the ladder in an organization, the further out that your thinking should be. You should have longer range planning. You will not attain your long-term goals over night so you must set yourself up with some short-term goals. These must be measurable and attainable for your team to be worth going after. These short-term milestones are what keep your team on task toward the end goal that you had in mind.

> **Habakkuk 2:2 (English Standard Version)**
>
> And the LORD answered me: "Write the vision; make it plain on tablets, so he may run who reads it.

Teach your team what your vision is. You have to have a true conviction to accomplish this. You have to be an inspiration to your followers. They can help develop the strategies to get there. Sure, you can get them started on that path. If they do not truly understand and support your vision, you do not have a team effort toward reaching your goals. What is part of the reason that you hire such a strong staff? I would assume that part of this is their intelligence. Why do some managers not want to tap into this valuable resource? Once your team has bought into your vision, they can probably give you the insight as to numerous ways that you can get to that same result. Sometimes, you will make your company more money. In other cases, it might make your company a safer company to work for. I will give you an example later on how this enhanced my overall customer service at a store that I worked at.

I have always taken the approach that those working the front line have a better working knowledge of how to do the job better than I do. They are the ones that do it day after day. They will know how to be more efficient. They know what is needed to make the job safer. All you need to do is ask them. Think outside the box. Just because it is always been done one way does not mean that it always has to be done that way. Your team has a wealth of knowledge. You need to learn how to use it. This is a huge motivator. When your team has input into your systems and procedures they end up with total buy in. It is now their vision, not just yours. They will put more effort into programs that they have put into place than those that were just given to them.

Although leadership is often associated with people in management positions, note that the two are not necessarily synonymous. A manager is someone who plans and administers a group's activities. Managers often focus on the bottom line of an organization, relying on control to accomplish their goals. In comparison, a leader is someone who is confident enough to take a different approach. They think outside the box and are thinking more long-term. They are not thinking about just short term results. They are in it for the long haul and approach their team this way. Effective leaders focus on building strong relationships with others and maintain their positions by inspiring trust and confidence in other members of the group. This takes time. It does not happen overnight.

These attributes of a strong leader are what helps build relationships with people. These strong relationships, if channeled right, turn into a strong team. The performance of the team in achieving the goals is reflective of the type of leader that is in the center of the team. Notice that I said center of the team, not in charge of the team. It is crucial that you're part of the team. You must be willing to jump in and work side by side with them. That is how you develop respect. So as you see, there are management skills that are needed by a strong leader and leadership skills needed to be a strong manager.

I told you earlier how I started my career. I wanted to be a successful manager. I needed that control and the feeling of being in charge. I worked with my employees to a certain extent, but my main focus was they were there to take care of my needs. The needs of the business always outweighed the needs of the individuals. I always made money for the company. I always pushed the limits of what we could do. Too often it was at the expense of employees. It took me awhile to figure out how much better I could be, if I concentrated on been a strong leader instead of being just a strong manager.

Chapter Two
Qualities of a Strong Leader

You can not take this guidance from The Lord lightly. As a leader of a group or organization, you affect many components and lives. God wants us to become strong leaders and to do so require the right approach. It all comes down to how we treat people. The Bible teaches us these principles in a wide variety of situations.

> Romans 12:8 (New Living Translation)
>
> . . . . If God has given you leadership ability, take the responsibility seriously. . . . .

I have seen patterns in the biblical teachings that I have read. They are scattered throughout the Old and New Testament. As you go through this book, I will go into more detail about the different expectations of how we can be a better leader. Here are the qualities that every leader should have.

- Be a Good Listener

- Be Responsive

- Be Respectful

- Show Compassion

- Be Understanding

- Empower Your Team

- Be Trustworthy

What is God really telling us to do? Sometimes when we read Bible verses, it is very easy to comprehend exactly what God wants from us. In other cases we have to translate it into our own lives. There are many things that are different about the world now as compared to when Jesus walked the earth. The way that you treat people the right way should be the same no matter when the time. So much of being a strong leader is how you interact with others. How does He want us to approach this leadership role that we have taken on? When I read the Bible, these are the traits that I see that are preferred by God. Let us look at these a little closer and find their roots in the Bible.

BE A GOOD LISTENER

Have you ever been talking to someone and they got so passionate about what they were talking about that it comes off pretty rude? They are so emotional about what they called you about on the phone that they hardly let you speak. Shortly after the conversation starts you close off your mind to what they are saying and form an opinion about the subject without really hearing their side of the story? How can you begin to relate to what they are saying if you are blocking them out? Sometimes they realize that you are blocking them out and that gets them upset. At that point the conversation really goes down hill.

Your friends will generally forget about that awkward conversation quickly. Your team members may not. If they are passionate about something and bring it to your attention, it deserves your undivided attention. You need to concentrate on what they are saying. Listen for what point they are trying to get across and not just how they are saying it. Listen for things like frustration, road blocks, struggles, etc., that are preventing them from being successful. If you listen closely enough, you can start to help them out. They may just need some assistance from a coworker but did not realize that the help they needed was right in front of them.

I worked for a manager once that got so frustrated with a coworker because of the way she would vent frustrations. He would want her to just get things done and quit complaining. He did not want to "deal" with her. There was no patience or tolerance of this behavior. When I listened to her, I filtered out the words of frustration. I did not listen to how she said it, but why she had that frustration. In one situation she was lacking some tools of the job to be able to complete the task. Her raised voice and not so eloquent language was hiding the truth. It took an extra effort of listening, including the unspoken words, to figure out the reason for the conversation.

There were things that she needed help with to be able to complete the tasks required of her. Her sense of pride did not let her ask for help. People tend to try to do it all themselves. They are too proud to ask for help. Here is an example from the Bible. Jesus is the Son of God. He is all powerful and all knowing. How could he possibly learn from someone else? As you can see in the scripture, He takes more of a humble approach to listening and learning. In turn, He could teach them along the way.

> ## Luke 2:45-47 (NIV)
>
> 45When they did not find him, they went back to Jerusalem to look for him. 46After three days they found him in the temple courts, sitting among the teachers, listening to them and asking them questions. 47Everyone who heard him was amazed at his understanding and his answers.

Jesus showed the importance of listening. This text talks about when Jesus was twelve years old. He slipped away from Mary and Joseph and went to the temple. He took the approach of a young boy with a lot of questions. Being the Son of God, He had the power to be the leader of all people. What this shows is that we have to grow to become true leaders. You do not just become a strong leader in a short amount of time. Part of the way that we grow is to listen to others. We need to absorb their wealth of knowledge. He was "taking it all in", so to speak. Twenty years later, when He was the Teacher, it showed that He had grown into being a true leader. Too often we feel as if we know it all and do not listen to what our coworkers are saying. Our arrogance blocks out a powerful gift from our team. They have so much knowledge that we could tap into. We can not only learn from others, but also build on our relationships with them by truly listening to what they have to say. We gain a few things by talking to our team and asking for their opinions. We will gain knowledge about the subjects through their point of view. This gives us insights as to how we may need to look at policies and procedures. We could possibly learn how to make our processes more efficient. One of the biggest values in doing this is the respect that shows your team. This respect goes a long way toward building a new relationship. I will go into the topic of respect in much more detail later in the book.

Too often we just take our listening skills for granted. Hearing we can somewhat take for granted. It is a natural ability. Truly listening to someone is more of an acquired skill. There are so many aspects that we do not pay attention to in our regular conversations. When someone speaks to you, they're not just saying words. They are communicating with the spoken words, nonverbal cues and their emotions. You need to be able to understand all of these and be able to process what they mean. Can you relate to what they're saying? Can you empathize with what they're feeling? When we listen to somebody, we do not just hear what they're saying. We normally hear background noises as well. Are they a distraction? Can we give that person our undivided attention? No two people think exactly the same way. That is why sometimes it is hard for people to understand what we're saying to them.

A perfect example of this is men and women. The way men think is completely different than the way women think. Sometimes this difference drives us crazy. You may think that you have the other sex figured out, but then you're thrown for a loop. What happens is that you make assumptions to what the other person is trying to communicate. You already have your next thought planned out. That is what gets men into trouble with their wives at times. They just "do not get it." What they think is "no big deal" turns out is extremely important to their spouse. When they say that they do not really want anything for their birthday, you may need to think it through. I have had my share of "misunderstandings" with women over the years. I now know that I will never figure them out.

When you do not take the time to truly understand what the other person he is saying and feeling they feel that you do not respect them. If you are unsure as to what they're saying or feeling, then ask them. You may paraphrase what they just said to see if that's what they meant. Or you can ask them to rephrase what they just said because you don't truly understand them. Do not abruptly change the subject. By doing that it looks like you're not listening what they were saying. It looks like you were already thinking about the next thing that you want to talk about and not listening to what they are saying. A big part of being a good listener is about being respectful.

BE RESPONSIVE

Now that you have listened to what they have to say, what do we need to do next? How are you going to respond to what they had to say? Did the person need to have you take some action? Sometimes they do not specifically tell you that they needed to do something. You have to understand what they're saying and the perceptive to their needs. They may have shown a concern about a particular area of the job. They may need some help or need some follow-up on how to do something. If they have basically called you to action, then you need to act. That will show how trustworthy you are. If you just ignore their requests, how does that make them feel?

Be careful how you respond. I'm sure that you have seen many approaches to how managers respond to their teams. Think back about some of the people that you've worked for. I am sure that you have seen many types of styles. Do they even take the time to respond to their team when asked a question? Do they give an honest response to the question asked? Do they come across as being irritated because of even being asked the question? People take many approaches to how they respond to people. Is there a right way and a wrong way? Let us let the Bible give us some insight.

> Proverbs 15:1 (New Living Translation)
>
> A gentle answer turns away wrath, but a harsh word stirs up anger

This talks about the way we answer people. God does not always give us the answers that we want to hear. He does, however, give us an answer. Do not tell someone that you will get back to them and then hope that they will forget about it. Tell them "no, I can not provide this at this time", if that is all that is possible. Be sympathetic to their struggles if you can not provide everything that they want at this time. The key is to be upfront and honest with them enough to give them a response. Sometimes you're caught off guard or you do not have the answer for somebody at that given point in time. Let them know that. Explain to them, if needed, that you need to do some more research and get back to them. Do not hesitate. Do the research that you need to do and then get back to them with an answer. This also shows respect.

I have seen managers that appeared to take the approach that if they ignored a problem, it would go away. No matter what was brought up regarding it, they would not respond. Phone calls and e-mails would be used to bring it to their attention with no response at all. Phone calls would not be returned. E-mails would go unanswered. Eventually the staff would give up and quit bothering them. In their minds, the problem is now solved. Did the problem go away? In most cases, it got worse. People communicate with one another. If they have frustrations, they will vent to their peers. This could be in the break room over a cup of coffee. It could be while they're outside smoking a cigarette with somebody from another department. Eventually they will talk to somebody about it. Now, what started out being a simple request or question is beginning to turn into a big issue.

To the manager, on the surface it appeared to work. The problem was no longer discussed in front of them. They no longer get the phone calls or e-mails. On the other hand, the management lost respect and created a much larger problem. All it would have taken was a response. Human nature is to avoid confrontation. We tend to not want to tell someone bad news. Avoidance, though, is not the answer. We need to be willing to take a different approach. Be upfront and honest with your staff. Most of your staff is going to understand that you have a business to run. They're going to be some things that you just can not afford to give them. An honest approach to them does not cost you anything. You may not always tell them what they want to hear. You have to be the bearer of bad news. It may be that they want you to make an exception to a rule for them. Sometimes it is something that they want that you can not afford to get for them. Rumors get started over different topics all of the time. You may have team members that ask you very direct questions. Sometimes I have to tell my staff "this is a subject that I am not at liberty to discuss." Your responsiveness is also a sign of your respect for them.

A while back, I needed to meet with an employee about a bonus program that was in place. He had questions about how it worked. After I explained it to him, he proceeded to argue with me over the policy. I sympathized with him based on how he was affected, but had to be willing to defend the company policy. I could not waiver since we had carried out the policy consistently in all cases. In the end, we had to "agree to disagree." How do you think that he would have responded if I had not taken the time to discuss it further with him? He probably would have had all sorts of negative things to tell his peers regarding the management of the company. It is crucial that you respond to your staff.

BE RESPECTFUL

How does it make you feel when you are not respected? Are the words that you say and do the actions that you take show respect for your co-workers? Too often it is the unspoken words that get us in trouble. We can go back to the topic of listening. Are you a respectful listener or do you always interrupt to get your thoughts into the conversation? Put yourself in their shoes. What is currently on their mind? What are they feeling?

The unspoken word goes a long way toward building up or tearing down a relationship. Really look at your approach and try to see it from their perspective. Are you self centered? Try putting them in the center of attention for all the good reasons. What can you do to raise their ego and self confidence? I have taken a lot of personality tests over the years. I completed one the other day that asked around three hundred questions. I was getting frustrated because it just kept going on forever. Many of the questions were just another way to word a previous question. One question that was asked in a few different ways was "Do you see the good in people or the bad?" It is kind of like the "glass half full or half empty" approach to life. You will see more good in people if you treat them respectfully.

Now that you are looking for some of the good in

people, let them know what you see. Compliment them in front of their peers. It goes a long way. I was told by a close friend early on in life that giving flowers to your loved one means more if you send them to their work. It shows the people that they work with how special they are to you. Just bringing them home is not as special. They do not have the ability to show them off. What it comes down to is that they want to be shown off to their peers.

It is not good enough to treat the people that we like with respect. We should treat everybody with respect. This is why it is one of the Ten Commandments.

> Mark 12:31 (NIV)
>
> The second is this: 'Love your neighbor as yourself.' There is no commandment greater than these."

In the New Testament, "agape" is the word most often used to describe Christian love. It is the love that comes from the Holy Spirit. It is the kind of love that Jesus had when he died for us on the cross. This shows us how we should treat others. It is unconditional. We should have this type of love for everyone around us. This even applies to those people that we work with or come in contact with throughout the day that "get on our last nerve" or are not polite and respectful to us. It should not make a difference where they come from or the type of person that they are. A good example of this in the Bible is the story of the Good Samaritan. A man was traveling from Jerusalem to Jericho. Along the way he was attacked by robbers and beaten. A priest passed by, traveling the same way. He did not stop to help the man, but instead, passed on the other side of the road. Then there was the Levite who came across the same gentleman. He too, passed on the other side of the road. When the Samaritan saw the injured gentlemen, he stopped to help. He helped bandage up his wounds and took him to get more help. He showed agape love, by doing this. It did not matter to him where the person was from or what religion he was. He was just interested in helping his fellow man.

We need to take the same approach. We need to treat everybody with respect, unconditionally. It seems like an easy concept to grasp. We know how we want to be treated. Why is it so hard to treat other people that way? We tend to interrupt conversations because we're in a hurry and want to take care of our business right away. We do not have the patience to wait until the other conversation is done before interrupting. We expect people to drop what they are doing and take care of our needs. Put yourself in the other person's shoes. They now have to stop what they're doing to take care of you. Does that show any respect for the conversation that they were in the middle of or the project that they were working on? Another way that we tend to be disrespectful is to talk about people behind their backs. Does it make us feel better about ourselves when we can put somebody else down? Let me give you an example. Have you ever been in a situation where you're sitting around talking with coworkers and someone makes a comment about another coworker? They make remarks about the person's lack of intelligence or their weight or their age. They think it's funny so they tell a little joke. What is your response? Do you jump in and add another joke? Do you just sit there, smile and not say a word? Does that show respect for the person that they're talking about? What if it were you that they were talking about and you are not in the room? If you heard about it, how would you feel?

My weight has gone up and down over the years. I can see it. I do not need somebody to point it out to me. It has been a struggle for me. There's no reason for anyone other than my doctor, to say something about it. Other people have their own self conscience issues. We see things throughout the day, every day that we know are disrespectful. The main thing is to learn from those experiences and to try to improve ourselves in how we treat others.

There are so many ways that we can be respectful. Some of it falls under just common courtesy. Some of these fall under the law. We cannot discriminate due to race, sex, age and religion, to name a few. How many times do we prejudge somebody just by the way that they look or act? I'm sure that you have seen some of the talent shows on TV. There have been a few examples of people that did not sing the way that we envisioned them in our minds. There have been some tremendous opera singers that when they were through auditioning we thought to ourselves "I did not see that coming." We tend to have stereotyped people.

SHOW COMPASSION

What is showing respect or not showing respect say about you? Does that reflect your true feelings towards others? What are people's perceptions about you? Do you care about your employees and does it show? I am sure that you have worked for a boss that did not care. All of us have at one point or another in our life. It was all about getting the job done and them getting ahead regardless of the costs. Chances are you have had this type of boss somewhere in your career. There are a lot of them out there.

These are the ones that are going to get ahead no matter whoever they have to step on to get there. It is a very aggressive approach. I know it because I used to be this way. How did it make you feel? Remember your coworkers and possibly yourself talking about the boss behind their back about what a tyrant they were. Did it motivate you to do a better job and to do extra to help the team succeed? I do not think so.

> Colossians 3:12-13 (NIV)
>
> Therefore, as God's chosen people, holy and dearly loved, clothe yourselves with compassion, kindness, humility, gentleness and patience. Bear with each other and forgive one another if any of you has a grievance against someone. Forgive as the Lord forgave you.

Compassion is a feeling that you experience when you

truly care about someone who is suffering. It is when you feel sorry for them and would do anything to help them. It is easy for us to have compassion when we talk about our loved ones. If our children are going through a hard time, we feel for them. We would do anything for them. Can we say the same for the people that we work with? Suffering can take on numerous meanings. Most of the time that we think about compassion is when we discuss somebody's health. They could be struggling in other areas of their life. It could be relationships at home. It could be finances. They could be struggling at work. Their work schedule might not be working with everything going on in their personal life at this time. They could be struggling with coworkers and not getting along. Do you care about any of this going on in their lives? Would you rather them to keep their personal stuff to themselves and just get on with work?

Earlier in my career, I was managing a full service restaurant. It was a busy Friday night and I was working in the kitchen. Because of budget cutbacks, the general manager had the evening off. It was a struggle. The company was not doing well financially. We had to trim back our management staff. There were only two managers at that restaurant. We had a lead server that could assist in running a shift. The only way that we got a day off was for the other manager to work a double shift. This was my double shift. I had the shift leader working the dining room that evening. The kitchen staff was falling behind on the orders. The dining room was full of guests. Our wait time at the hostess stand was approximately 45 minutes for a guest to get a table. I decided to jump in on the grill cook line and assist the cooks. We could not afford to get further behind. I was frustrated with my team at that point. They were not handling the rush the way that I felt like they could. I lost my patience.

Because of my frustration, I got in too big of a hurry. When trying to blacken a steak, I rushed and forgot to empty the butter in the pan from the previous order. I threw the steak into the pan and the grease hit the back wall of the frying pan and flew back into my face. I told the staff to call the general manager at home and inform him of the situation. He would need to cover for me while I went to the hospital. I was there for probably about an hour and a half. I had second degree burns on my face. The upper half of my white shirt and tie were black from grease. The doctor wrote me an excuse to be off work for three days to allow my face to heal. I came back to the restaurant and could feel the heat of the kitchen on my face as soon as I walked in the door. I was greeted by the general manager. He did not ask me how I was doing. He let me know that he had brought me a clean white shirt and tie so I could finish the shift and he was going home. I was speechless. How was that for compassion? You may not have had a manager treat you exactly this way. This was probably not his intent to come across that way. Look at your actions. They are a reflection of how you feel. Your actions will show your employees how you feel about them. I knew immediately that night how the manager felt. I had ruined his Friday night off.

Would you go the extra mile for this person? I would not. From that day forward, I would tend to do just enough. I would do my own thing and stay out of the way. I was not about to go the extra mile to make him look better. In this case, my resume was updated the following morning. Within six months, I was working for another company. On the other hand, I have had managers that truly cared about my well being and I would do most anything for them. I would dig in and help the team exceed their goals and expectations. Isn't this what you would like to accomplish?

You do not have to get intimately involved in every aspect of your coworker's lives, but being there as a listener to their concerns and struggles that they are going through goes a long way. Show some empathy and compassion for what they're going through. You may not be able to help them other than just to listen to them. Then, the next time you are in conversation with God, lift up that person and what is going on so He can lay a comforting hand on them and help them through it. This is one of the greatest gifts that you can give to somebody. It is the gift of prayer.

BE UNDERSTANDING

This leads me to understanding people. Don't just listen to the words that they say, but the thoughts and ideas that they are trying to convey. It may be struggles with some processes that you have put into place for their job. Try to understand what is going on in their situation. Try to gain some knowledge from the situation. Without this understanding, you are foolish.

> **Proverbs 15:21 (English Standard Version)**
>
> Folly is a joy to him who lacks sense,
> but a man of understanding walks straight ahead.

I earlier referred to a situation with the coworker of mine. Her manager was giving her a hard time for not turning in a report on time. He felt like the information that she needed for the report was easy to get to and there was no reason that she should have delayed completing it. I did not hear her conversation with him. I feel as though she probably did not use the appropriate words to describe the situation. She vented her frustrations. To him, she came across as being insubordinate. I was brought into the loop to try to resolve the situation. I listened to what she was saying and not just how she said it. I could hear the frustration in her voice. I got down to the root of her problem with completing the task. She lacked some computer training that would have made the job so much easier. She could not figure out how to do it and was too proud to admit. I went into her file and reformatted it so that she could get the answers that she was looking for. At that point, it was easy for her to complete the report.

Do not be so arrogant that you feel that the way that you are having them do something is the only way that the task can be accomplished. Be open to suggestions of improvement. It not only gives your team a greater sense of ownership in the process, but it will probably improve your business along the way. This may be in the form of efficiencies, reduction of errors or safety. Put yourself in their shoes. You have to understand where they are coming from. How and why do they have the perspective that they do? People come from different backgrounds. They have different experiences in life. Because of these reasons, no two people think completely alike. Part of the understanding people is listening to them as we discussed earlier. They did take into consideration there nonverbal cues as well as what they're saying to you. If you do not fully grasp the concept that they're talking about, then you need to ask them to clarify.

I felt like an idiot the other morning during our church service. I alternate with another person in operating our sound system for our praise worship service. It was my week to run the soundboard. The praise team had just started singing as people were coming into the sanctuary. I was concentrating on getting the volume balanced for the vocals. An elderly lady came up to me and asked for assistance. She spoke softly and I struggled to understand what she was talking about. What I heard was "I am looking for a good place to sit." I pointed out some available pews. I was in a hurry to get back to the sound board. I knew that I was short on time and that the pastor would begin to speak shortly. I would need to turn on his microphone. I did not mean it this way, but what I was telling this woman was that I did not have time to deal with her. It showed through in what I said and how I said it. I realized quickly what I had just done. I then put my ear up closer to her and asked her to repeat what she needed. It was at that point that I understood that she was trying to find her son. She pointed from the balcony down to the lower level to an area where her son normally sat. She asked me if I knew him and gave me his name. At this point, I knew that I was out of time. I also knew that I needed to give her assistance.

I told her to wait right there as I went to get some help. Some neighbors of mine were close to that area of the sanctuary. I knew that they knew many people in the church and could possibly know her son. I quickly explained to them her dilemma and I asked if they could help her so that I can get back to the sound board. They were unable to locate her son but offered to have her sit with them through the church service. They were a blessing to me that day as well as to this lady. This may not have turned out so well if I had not taken the time to truly understand what her needs were. Think about a situation you have been in where you have not taken the time truly understand what the other person was saying because you did not have time to deal with them.

EMPOWER YOUR TEAM

With understanding of what value your team has comes empowerment. Give them the ability to make decisions throughout the process. Do not make it so that they have to follow a strict set of rules and regulations and there is no deviance regardless of the situation. Teach them the rationale and purpose of the directions. What are your ultimate goals? If they understand that, then they can take it upon themselves to do what it takes to achieve them. Your staff needs to have the power to make decisions. They need the power to make things happen.

The Book of Acts in the Bible, tells us about the start of

the church. It is when Jesus, before He ascended into heaven, promised that the disciples would be given the power of the Holy Spirit. He told them that they would have to wait for it. They had to be patient. Too often we want everything now. We are not patient enough to wait for things. They had to stay in Jerusalem and wait for this gift of the Holy Spirit. That filling of them with the Holy Spirit is the empowerment that they needed. It gave them the power to go out and preach the teachings of Jesus. It is the same as giving your employees the tools needed to do a job. I am not just talking about physical tools. I am referring to the mental tools. It is the ability to think on their own to come up with decisions when needed to fulfill your vision. The disciples were told to go out into the world and tell everyone about the resurrected Christ and the promise of eternal life. That was the goal/vision that Jesus had for them. God's Kingdom is the ultimate vision and goal in life. We are so blessed with this promise that we should share it around the world. The power that we have to do this is the Holy Spirit within us. The Holy Spirit has empowered me to write this book. I may be driving home from work in the evening and I suddenly think of an experience that I can put down in the book that demonstrates one of the topics. I believe this is The Holy Spirit working inside of me.

> Acts 1:8 (NIV)
>
> But you will receive power when the Holy Spirit comes on you; and you will be my witnesses in Jerusalem, and in all Judea and Samaria, and to the ends of the earth

Leaders do not actually give their followers power. They enable them to have the power by the situations that they are put into. They are given the authority and the tools needed to obtain the power. Jesus had been coaching these disciples for three years before He empowered them with the Holy Spirit. He did not send them out on their own right away. There was a lot of training and eventual empowerment that got them ready. Look back at how we train people. They get a week, three months, or when we are desperate for help, three hours of training. I am sure that you have experienced this rush job of training. How did it work out? How did the new employee fair if they decided to keep working for you after the first few weeks? How can they possibly be able to handle the responsibility of empowerment in that short amount of time compared to the three years that Jesus gave the disciples? You need to invest your time and efforts into your team.

I have worked in restaurant management for the majority of my career. Picture a restaurant server that is asked by a customer if they can get a variation of their meal that was not listed in the menu. If you had not empowered them to take care of the customer, their answer might have been "I am sorry, but that option is not available". The customer would have then ordered something else or just settled for what was available. Now let's look at the empowered server. They would have taken it upon themselves to work with the cook to satisfy the customer's request. Ultimately, the client walks away with an exceptional experience and becomes a regular customer and promotes your business in the conversations with friends. The unsatisfied customer will also talk about your business to their friends, but not in the same light. Give them the mission to accomplish. In this case it was an exceptional dining experience and empowers them to make it happen.

Don Vlcek was the president of Domino's Pizza Distribution Corporation in the 1980s and 90s. They were the main supplier of the Domino's Pizza stores. I learned a lot about how to lead people from Don. He created a vision for the company that was bought in to by the majority of the employees that work for him.

One approach was having "team members that could not think of a better company to work for." He was constantly soliciting feedback from those who worked with him. He did not take the approach that he knew it all.

He developed a bonus program that included every member of the staff. Every one who worked in a commissary/distribution center had the same goals. When the commissary achieved its goals, everybody received a bonus. Your bonus level was determined by your position with the company, but it was always paid out based on the same criteria as the rest of the people on the team. This unified the team. It kept the team focused on the same goals. They are all going in the same direction. One of the biggest goals that we had at that time was to not have a pizza store close because of running out of product. There was no operations manual to tell you what you needed to do to prevent a store from closing. You just knew that you had to do anything in your power to make this a reality. If you failed, you let your whole team down. It may be due to the dough production team dropping the ball. That would cost the truck driver and office staff their bonus as well.

I remember, on occasions, taking pizza dough to the airport and putting it on a plane to fly to another state so that they would not run out of dough to work with. Not once did we think about how much it would cost to get it sent. We just knew that we could not afford to have that store close because we can not get them dough. Sometimes stores were only a couple hours away from our commissary. I knew how many trays of dough I could put into my Ford Escort. One day I was working in Fort Worth and heard that a store in Oklahoma City needed product right away. I packed up the Ford full and headed down the road. I got there in time but had to have a friendly chat with a police officer along way. He felt that since I could not see out of my mirrors that I had cut him off. It seemed logical at the time since I could not know for sure if I had cut him off are not. The whole passenger seat was full and I could not see out of the mirrors. I took my ticket and headed on to my destination. The store did not close but I also knew in the future that I had to be more careful. We were determined to accomplish this goal no matter what the cost. This was just one scenario. You could never have an operation manual or micromanage to the point that you had every situation written on how to act in a crisis. This level of empowerment to the staff to do what it needed to do to reach the goals was what made it all successful.

It all came down to the vision. The whole team had ownership in the vision. We were empowered to make decisions. It reminds me of the phrase "It is easier to ask for forgiveness than to ask for permission." As long as we were following the plan and accomplishing the goals, the decisions along the way were not questioned. They evaluate the situations afterwards and determine if there may have been a better way to accomplish it in the future, but no one ever got in trouble for making a decision that solved the problem.

BE TRUSTWORTHY

Are you true to your word? I used to joke with some of the people that I have worked with about telling the client or potential client everything that they wanted to hear. There would be all sorts of promises made that person knew could not be fulfilled. They figured that they would figure out a solution or they just would not fulfill the promises and hope that the client would not come back and ask about it. A situation from fifteen years ago comes to mind. I was managing a cafeteria and was promoted to run all of the cafeterias in the district. In the upcoming months, I had two things to take care of. I had to train my assistant manager to take over the operations of that cafeteria. I also had to go to the other four cafeterias and supervise those teams as well. Our client at that location kept close tabs on the cafeteria operation. My supervisor did not want her to lose confidence in the operation during this transition period. Because of this, I would start my day at this location. Sometime during the morning I would head out to the other cafeterias but always made sure that I was back around lunchtime. This way she would not see that I was gone for very long at a time. I was told to tell my team that if she asked where I was, they were supposed to tell her that I was going to the bank to buy change. After a few weeks, my conscience could not take it anymore. I met with her to discuss the overall situation. I explained to her that I had been promoted and that the manager that was taking over for me was extremely competent. She had no problems with that at all. Looking back at this, I wish that I had been completely honest from the beginning. What do you think her trust in me would have been like if she had found out what was going on before I had met with her?

Solomon wrote the Book of Proverbs in the Bible. He was teaching the young people of his day the important things of life and how to obtain wisdom. He was showing them how to lead a proper life. He was teaching them how to apply God's wisdom to their lives. Part of what he taught them was about personal relationships. That may be in the form of friends, coworkers and family. This includes been trustworthy.

> Proverbs 12:22 (New Living Translation)
>
> The LORD hates those who don't keep their word, but he delights and those who do.

Does this describe you? Are you one that makes all sorts of promises just to make someone happy and do not worry about living up to your commitments? I have always believed in under promising and over delivering. There may be a request that I think that I may be able to do, but have a certain level of doubt whether or not I can do it. I try to let the person know that it is my goal to satisfy their request, but I need to do more research or brainstorming for ideas of how to make it happen. Notice that I did not ignore their request, but was honest in my approach.

One of the first things about being trustworthy is for people to believe that you will do what you promise to do. They trust that if you say you're going to do something, then you will. Another way that we trust somebody is to know that they're not going to lie, cheat or steal from us. Are they going to be honest? One other area is whether or not they believe that they can give you a task and you will give it all of your effort to accomplish that task. These are all things that they taught us in grade school. How do things like this get away from us as we get older? Why do we let our values slip? Are we influenced too much by those around us? We need to get back to our spiritual upbringing. We have to stay true to our values.

Chapter Three
What Defines Your Leadership Style?

How much control do we have over our leadership style? What can we do to influence that style? These three key items define most people's leadership style.

- Personality

- Values

- Integrity

These are the core items that define our leadership style. They are the elements that determine how and why we lead the way that we do. Let us look at each one individually.

PERSONALITY

What is personality? Merriam-Webster says: the complex of characteristics that distinguishes an individual or a nation or group; *especially*: the totality of an individual's behavioral and emotional characteristics

Have you heard people say that one person has a great personality and another one has a horrible personality? What do they really mean? Everyone's personality is different from each other. Some are quite similar, while others are quite different. Have you noticed that someone from the north has a different personality than someone from the south? They say that if you grew up in a small town in the south, you have never met a stranger. Up north, in a big city, you would never think to say hello to a stranger while walking down the street. We talk about some people having an outgoing personality while others do not. Some people are very quiet and prefer to be alone than to be mingling in a group. There are some that will give you their opinion on things even if you do not want to hear it. There are others that will never share their opinion because they do not want to offend others or they feel that their opinions do not matter.

Now think about your own circumstances. How were you raised? How do people perceive your personality? Sometimes their first impression of you is not really your true personality. People see me as "a laid back" manager. I do not get emotionally worked up very often. Some of them feel that because of this personality, I'm not strict with my team. Once they get to know me though, they see that I hold high standards for the people who work for me. This is my personality now, but it has evolved over the years. I am not telling you to change your personality. You do not really have control over that. It is in your nature and upbringing. You need to realize it helps define who you are and how you lead people. You need to be aware of your personality. You can influence how people perceive you based on the other attributes of a good leader presented throughout this book. Their perception of you dictates a lot of how successful you will be.

You also need to know the personalities of the people on your team. This is going to influence your approach to them as well. We can not take a cookie cutter approach to developing a team. Not everything that you do motivates everyone else. Are you self centered or are you a good listener? Pay attention to your conversations with friends and coworkers over the next week. Do you do most of the talking or are you the listener? Do the topics end up being yours or the person who you are talking with? Most people are not really aware of the true aspects of their conversations. Most of the time, we're not necessarily listening to what we are saying. All we hear is what we're saying and are not always aware of all the nonverbal cues that are associated with it.

This is part of your personality coming through. Focus on really listening to what the other person has to say. Do not start thinking of the next topic before they are through. It insults me when I finish speaking about something expecting a response to what I just said and the other person is already moving onto something going on in their life and changing the subject. This shows them how much you care about them. It is disrespectful to dominate all conversations. What does it say about your compassion for the person? Do you really care about them or is it always about you? If you are trying to develop a strong team, everyone needs to take the spot light at sometime or another. Make them feel worthy of your respect and interest.

Respect goes a long way. How do you treat others? I have heard people say that you have to earn people's respect. I take that approach with myself. I do not expect someone to respect me from the start without knowing me. I do feel, though, that you need to treat people with respect from the beginning. That seems as if I contradict myself, but let me explain.

How much patience do you have? That is part of your personality. I know that you have worked with others that are very patient and some that have no patience at all. We all have. How did you feel about each of these approaches? I am not talking about tolerance? Some people do not tolerate inexcusable behavior and it comes across as being impatient. I am talking about the kind of patience that shows through when one person does not pick up a task as quickly as the rest and your approach to that person. Do you take the time to figure out their situation and how you can assist them in learning the new task? Do you "kick them to the curb" and find someone else to do the job? Do you put yourself in other's shoes in situations or is it "all about you" and your needs that you are concerned about? I am starting to see pattern here, are you?

So much of how we interact with others is based on

our personality. If we could just picture ourselves through other people's eyes we may learn something about ourselves. We could learn why we do some of the things that we do and may be able to slowly change our thought processes. There have been quite a few personality tests that have been developed over the years. The most highly trusted one of all is the Myers-Briggs Type Indicator©. The Myers-Briggs Type Indicator© is the culmination of years of research by Katherine Briggs and her daughter Isabel Briggs Myers. I recently took the test along with our management staff at a company wide meeting. We were amazed at the results and how accurately it described us. The test evaluates how we perceive things and therefore how we judge things.

The way that the test describes your personality falls under these main traits. Extraversion, Introversion, Sensing, Intuition, Thinking, Feeling, Judging and Perceiving. By determining your tendencies toward different traits, this test will categorize you into one of sixteen different personality types. As we looked at the category that each of us fell into, we could immediately think back of different occasions that we applied these personality traits in making our judgments and decisions. Go to their website, https:www.myersbriggs.org, to find out more about this test. It proved to me that our personality traits strongly influence our leadership style.

VALUES

Your personal values are based on the circumstances that you have been exposed to. How you were raised? How did your parents' values influence your life? Do you have the same values as they or have you developed your own based on your opinions of their values? Religious beliefs, culture and political views have an impact on what type of person you are. They are all going to play a role in the way that you approach people. They affect how you lead people.

Some of our values in life are taught to us by our parents. I've been blessed with two great parents. I can honestly say that they raised me right. They taught me the value of a day's work. I learned the importance of doing things together as a family. They showed me what I needed to be trustworthy and honest. One of those lessons that they taught me I remember well. As a young boy growing up in a small town, I was riding my bicycle to the small grocery store at the edge of town to buy some candy. My mom would give us some money to buy some penny candy and it may have been 25¢ each time we went to the store. I would load up the small brown paper bag of candy and feel like I hit the lottery. I would not even think about using 10¢ of it for a candy bar when I could get ten pieces of candy instead. On this particular location as I was leaving the store doing what many kids did then and maybe still do. I went to the soda machine and checked to see if anyone forgot to pick up the change from the coin slot. I also hit the buttons on the vending machine to see if a drink would fall out. I do not know what made me try that. It never worked until this time. To my surprise a can of soda came out of the machine. I was so happy. Not only did I have a bag of candy, I also had a nice cold drink to sip on for the ride home.

When I got home, my mom asked me where I got the soda. She knew how much money she had given me and knew that I did not have 25¢ to purchase it. I, not being aware that I did anything wrong, calmly explained what I had done. Next, she taught me the lesson that has stuck with me my whole life. She told me that I would have to go back to the store and give the cashier the money for the drink. I justified my opinion of not needing to do this because it was from the vending machine and not inside the store. It also seemed as though someone else had already paid for it or it would not come out when the button was pushed. That was not the right answer. Mom told me that "I" had not paid for it which means that I stole it. With that logic, she gave me a quarter to take back to the store. I was so embarrassed to go back to the clerk and explain my dilemma. I told her the whole situation because she questioned why I was trying to pay for a drink that she had not sold me. She was polite and probably felt sorry for me and told me that she did not want my quarter. The apology for taking the drink was fine in her mind. I insisted that she take the money. I knew that I could not go home with the quarter in my pocket and look mom in the eyes and say that I had paid for the drink.

Our values are a combination of a life long journey. There are examples along the way that are good and bad. We need to take advantage of these lessons and learn from them.

Your values can change over time based on circumstances. Are you easily swayed in your beliefs? Some people are set in their ways and no matter what goes on around them; they will not change their values or beliefs. Your highest priorities that are deeply held inside of you are the values that define you the most. Are you true to those values? This is where I differed in my approach to leadership than some managers that I have worked with. My religious faith has defined these values and they are true in my heart. I am going to try my hardest to never waiver from them. Another word that you can use for values is morals. I have questioned the way some of my previous managers have run their businesses. I know that what they were doing to their employees was not against the law. It sometimes went against what I consider my moral code of ethics.

INTEGRITY

That story of me, as a young boy, shows how my parents helped shape my integrity. Looking back, it was a small event that made a big impact on me. Integrity is how you apply your values. Can you be trusted? What are your actions saying? You have heard the phrase, "actions speak louder than words". Do you "talk the walk" or "walk the talk?" Do not just say who you are through your words, but live it through your actions. Think about your approach to others. Can someone develop their own opinions, or do they just have to follow your orders? If you do not let them think on their own, you must not trust them. Give them the vision and let them help pave the road to getting to the final goal. Trust them the way that you want to be trusted yourself. One of the biggest areas that define employee satisfaction within an organization is the trust and confidence that they have with the upper management. The top levels of management need to be able to communicate clearly the goals of the organization. They must be able to create that vision and explain it well enough that the staff knows how they fit into that vision. They will then need to be able to express how their staff accomplished their objectives based on the direction of the leadership. If you are lacking the trust it will cause the staff to not believe in your vision and buy into the objectives set out in front of them. If they are lacking in confidence of you, they will lose confidence in themselves to reach the business objective set forth.

What is your word worth? Do people trust that what you tell them is always going to be the truth? Do you follow up with what you tell people you're going to do? Some people do not take this concept seriously enough. They make empty promises. They can not be counted on to follow through with what they said that they would do. These are all aspects of integrity.

> **James 5:12 (New King James Version)**
>
> But above all, my brethren, do not swear, either by heaven or by earth or with any other oath. But let your "Yes" be "Yes," and *your* "No," "No," lest you fall into judgment.

I have given some of the salespeople I have worked with over the years a hard time about this. It is a stereotype that you can not believe everything a salesperson tells you. They are just trying to sell you something. They will tell you anything that you want to hear. This may work one time, but how many times do you want to buy from the same salesperson if they are not telling the truth? We discussed earlier about being trustworthy. People need to trust that when we say we are going to do something, we will get it done. We are going to be honest with them at all times. There's no such thing as a little white lie. It is a lie. Do not try to justify it.

I believe in the philosophy of under promising and over delivering. What this means is that I do not make promises that I can not live up to. Sometimes people try to put pressure on me to make commitments that I know that I might not be able to make. I remember budget meetings like this. This does not mean that I am trying to make my job easy. I just want to be realistic. I do not want to give them any false hopes. Does that mean that I do not try to go over and above the normal expectations when working with clients? No, it means that if I feel like something may not be possible, I let the client know that up front. I explained to them that I will do everything in my power to make something happen but that there may be obstacles that I can not overcome. Some people call this "hedging your bet." I think that it is keeping my integrity intact. I had lunch with a client this past week. They wanted me to completely change up the way that we do our financial reporting to their company. At first thought, my reaction could have been, "sure, we can do that for you." What happens later down the road when I can not produce this new reporting in the way that they wanted it. I would lose all credibility. Instead, I explained to them that I would pursue that possibility of changing the reporting structure. I told them the downfalls of converting it over and committed to exploring the ins and outs of the conversion process. I would present it to our management team to see if it was something that we would consider or not. I did commit to timely reporting on their terms, which may involve estimates of costs on our end. We walked away from lunch with a clear understanding of where we would go from there. Be careful what you promise so that you can uphold your end of the agreement. Do not put your integrity at risk.

When I make a promise to somebody, I will do everything in my power to uphold that obligation. I want people to be able to count on me to do a job. If it is an area that I am not comfortable with or do not have the expertise in, then I may need to refer them to someone else. There is nothing wrong with this. No one is an expert on everything. I have catered for hundreds and thousands of people over the years. I do not have experience catering weddings. I have been asked numerous times over the years to cater someone's wedding. This is a special day in their lives. They deserve to have the best. Since I do not feel comfortable providing that for them, I do not feel bad about referring them to somebody else that I know they can take care of their needs. Sometimes you have to let loose of your pride and admit that you do not know it all.

Integrity is something that shines through in what you do. It is your code of ethics. If someone is always telling you about how ethical and honest that they are, I would begin to doubt them. If you have true integrity and a strong ethical base to your approach, your actions will speak for themselves. You will not need to talk about it. Let us get back to the little white lies. They are harmless (we think). "I had to lie to them, it was for their own good" is what we may say. What are your thoughts in these areas? Let us see what the Bible had to say about honesty.

> **Proverbs 11:3 (New Living Translation)**
>
> Good people are guided by their honesty; treacherous people are destroyed by their dishonesty.

> **Proverbs 20:7 (New Living Translation)**
>
> The godly walk with integrity; blessed are their children after them.

Your integrity is a virtue that you should strive for. You are on stage at all times. If it is truly in you, it will show through in your actions. Throughout this next week, pay attention to what you do. Think about what others are thinking about you. Are you true to your word? Did you tell a little white lie? Can people count on you to get a job done? Evaluate how you do it. Not take a look at it and figure out what you need to do going forward to improve in this area.

So your personality, values and integrity have molded you to what you are today. What does that mean in the big picture? What does it matter what your style of leadership is? Do people work differently because they work for you? I have talked to people about having a "bus plan" at work. I am not talking about the mass transit system. I mean, "How is your department going to run if tomorrow you were run over by a bus?" Are they going to have the skills and knowledge to keep going without you? Are you hoarding information and control so that they are completely reliant on you being there? Are they a better team from having worked with you? Will they continue to grow and be successful after you leave? Hopefully it is because you are promoted and not because you were run over by a bus. Be aware of what you are leaving behind. What kind of an impact, long term, have you had on this team?

Chapter Four
How does having God in the center of your life influence your style?

I have told you that my style of leadership has changed over the years. I can see a direct correlation between how close I was with God and how it affected the way that I managed. I noticed certain aspects of my leadership style that have change over the years. Here are some of the traits that I saw develop as I grew closer to God.

- Humility

- Patience

- Generosity

- Servant hood

• Compassion

You do not see a lot of these traits, in managers that are not strong leaders. They're too worried about obtaining power, leverage and control. It is all about them. They are the ones that are trying to get ahead. People around them are either stumbling blocks or just tools to help them get to where they want to be. I see this all the time around me. This was my reality for many years. I was one of these managers.

They are managers that are quick to take all the glory. They are ones that are quick to push off all the blame on to somebody else. I see it all of the time where a manager will not admit the first flaw in their leadership. They will never admit guilt if a problem arises. I do not know if it because they are insecure in their own talents that make them think that admitting errors would jeopardize their job. It may be that they feel that if someone knew that they messed up they would not carry as much respect. I think that by not admitting mistakes it shows arrogance and damages a person's reputation more than if they just said "I am sorry, I made a mistake. How can I fix it?"

HUMILITY

> Proverbs 11:2 (New Living Translation)
>
> Pride leads to disgrace, but with humility comes wisdom.

Part of being humble, is to admit that you have faults. There is nothing wrong with making mistakes. The problem is, when you deny that you ever make a mistake. Jesus died on the cross to forgive us of all our sins. We need to ask for forgiveness. Admitting that you make a mistake is crucial and the first step in the process of asking for forgiveness. Another way that I am humble is to admit that I do not know everything. I like to think that I'm willing to try to find the answer that somebody else needs. I do not have to have all of the answers. I just need to be willing to find the answers. The other people on my team have a lot of knowledge that I need to tap into. Part of being humble is to thank others for what they do.

You can never be too appreciative of others. People do not accomplish things on their own. Most of your accomplishments in life can be attributed in some way or another to somebody else. Somebody has helped you along the way. Somebody has given you advice. Your team has done something to make you look good. Take the time to think of them. Recognize what they've done. Redirect the praise that is given to you. If your team wins an award and you are the one recognized in front of a group, do not take all the credit. Be thankful for the award and redirect the accolades to your team. Make sure people know that it was a team effort that was successful.

You did not always have to be the first, the best, or always be right. Listen to people's suggestions. You're not an instant success. It took you a while to be as good as you are today. Someone helped to get you there. Someone coached you, guided you, and mentored you along the way. Be thankful for that. Recognize these people and remember them for what they've done for you.

PATIENCE

I have so much more patience now than I ever have. I am willing to accept that other people around me will make mistakes at times as well. It does not do me any good to beat them down and complain about their mistakes. I need to be willing to help them grow. They need to know about the mistakes, but be able to have the tools to be able to help avoid them in the future. I try to be a lot more forgiving now than when I had been in the past.

> **Psalm 37:7-9 (New Living Translation)**
>
> Be still in the presence of the LORD, and wait patiently for him to act. Don't worry about evil people who prosper or fret about their wicked schemes. Stop being angry! Turn from your rage! Do not lose your temper—it only leads to harm. For the wicked will be destroyed, but those who trust in the LORD will possess the land.

Our whole culture in this world has changed. We are in an "I want it now" environment. We're losing our patience Part of this is has been brought on by technology. Early in my career as a manager, I carried a pager with me. If someone was trying to get a hold of me and I was on the road, they would send me a page. It would give me a phone number of who I needed to call. They would have to wait patiently until I could get to a pay phone. Do they even make pay phones any more? The person trying to get a hold of me would know that it may take awhile for me to return a phone call. Now, with cell phones, everybody expects you to be available 100% of the time. We have the impression that if you have a cell phone there are no excuses for not answering it. Numerous times, a message is left to my voice mail saying "why are you not picking up?" I could be in a meeting. I could be on the phone, whether it is the cell phone or on a land line phone. We can not stand a waiting period. Everything needs to happen right now. I am sure that you have seen people answer their cell phones while in the rest room. Let's be realistic. There is nothing so important that it can not wait a few minutes.

Here is another way that this verse speaks to me. For many years I kept trying to get ahead. I was frustrated because some of the people that got ahead, whether it was getting promotions or by starting their business, they did so by doing things that went against my moral values. I kept questioning why it was that they could get ahead but I was left behind. It made me angry. It was not until I became patient, that I started to really succeed in business. When I quit worrying about what the next person was doing and just concentrated on my own works, I noticed a difference.

Sometimes patience is a hard trait to develop. The

stress in our lives sometimes triggers impatience. Then the impatience stirs up more stress. It turns into a vicious circle. People describe me as a very patient person. They also perceive me as not getting too stressed out over things. These two items, stress and impatience, go hand in hand. Impatience can compromise your ability to listen properly which could lead to damaged relationships both personally and professionally. Many of the effects of stress on your life can be reduced if you can develop your patience.

We need to apply this principle of patience in all aspects of our lives. You will notice a difference in your relationships at home and at work if you have patience with others. We need to increase the awareness of the patience level that we do have.

GENEROSITY

Generosity means so many things. Most of the time we think about generosity, we think about giving people or organizations money. We think about how we give a donation to our church or favorite charity. It could be how much time we have donated as a volunteer to a worthy cause. In the area of leadership,

I feel that it means giving some of your time, efforts or expertise to others. It means giving your constant support. Take the time to train others around you. Give them the tools of the job to be successful. If you have a strong knowledge of an area, you need to share it. When you are training somebody, use some of that patience. Not everyone is going to learn at the same speed. Give that person some of your patience and understanding so that they feel worth while in your organization. You need to be able to provide the same kind of skills by the end of a class to all of the participants. Some people may need a little bit more of your time, one on one. Do not be selfish and expect everybody to learn it at the same pace. Your team will be no stronger than your weakest person.

Once they have developed those skills, you need to give them the power to use them. Do not hold your team back from their potential. Let them develop and grow. Give everything in your power to nurture their growth. They are the future leaders in your organization. Lead with a generous heart.

SERVANT HOOD

Jesus taught us that the way that you were strong is by

being a servant. In the upper room, the disciples were battling over who would have the most power. They were simple men until Jesus came along. They wanted to tap into some of that influence that Jesus had to benefit their own stature in life. Jesus could have just put them in their place. I am sure that you have had a boss that did this a time or two. Jesus' approach was to get down on his knees and washed the feet of the disciples. It is obvious to us who had the most power in the room. It was Jesus. This symbolic gesture shows us the importance of serving your team. They are not just there to serve you. Think back to what you have done recently to serve your team. How did it make them feel? If you can not think of an example, use this time to be more aware of how you can better serve your team instead of just thinking about how they can serve you.

It says in the Bible that you must first be a servant before you can be a leader. You can learn so much from that perspective. Developing that sense of servant hood will take you far in the area of growing your leadership skills. Carrying that sense of servant hood in your leadership style plays a big part in developing a team.

> Matthew 20:26 (NIV)
>
> "Not so with you. Instead, whoever wants to become great among you must be your servant, and whoever wants to be first must be your slave just as the Son of Man did not come to be served, but to serve, and to give his life as a ransom for many."

It never ceases to amaze me how God leads my life. This morning, in my Sunday school class, we were studying in the book of John, chapter 21. This is a story about seven of the disciples during their time of waiting for Jesus to return to them. Jesus had already risen from the dead. This is one of the few times they would see Him in person before He ascended to Heaven. Peter convinced the disciples to go out fishing in the middle of the night. They were not having any luck catching any fish. Jesus appears to them on the shore. He instructed them to throw their nets over the other side of the boat. It was then, that they caught 153 fish. This is an example of His vision of them being fishers of men. When they came to shore with all their fish, Jesus had a fire going and was already cooking some fish. He asked them to bring in some of their fish and He fixed them breakfast. Here is the verse.

> John 21:12-13 (New Living Translation)
>
> "Now come and have some breakfast!" Jesus said. None of the disciples dared to ask him, "Who are you?" They knew it was the Lord. ¹³ Then Jesus served them the bread and the fish.

One of my classmates made an interesting observation. She said that while they were in the upper room and He washed their feet, He had not completely established Himself as their leader. Maybe it was not so odd that he served them by washing their feet at the time. Since then, He died and rose again. At this point, the disciples truly recognized Him as their leader. Once again, though, Jesus served them. This shows that while we are establishing our teams, we should be serving them. But also, when they are established, we should continue to serve them.

COMPASSION

I've developed more compassion over time. I used to not care what people thought or what was going on in their lives. It was all about my goal to get ahead. It did not matter to me what I had to do to, or with, people to get promoted. I see now, how ill-mannered I was in my ways. I now realize that it is my team and their performance that will get me ahead. I have to develop my team. They will not respect me or give me their best if I do not treat them with respect. Now I have a genuine concern about what goes on in their lives. I am trying to understand this. I can see how it affects their every-day work activities. I try to be more forgiving as God would want me to be. In this Bible translation, compassion is described as tenderhearted mercy.

> Colossians 3:12-13 (New Living Translation)
>
> Since God chose you to be the only people whom he loves, you must clothed yourselves with tenderhearted mercy, kindness, humility, gentleness, and patience. You must make allowances for each other's faults and forgive the person who offends you. Remember the lord forgave you, so you must forgive others.

Where do you go from here in applying some of these ideas? Maybe you have been faithful but God has played a background role in your life. You have tried to live a Christian life, but do not give it much thought throughout the day. Maybe what you need is a new attitude. You need to refocus on the important things in life. Putting God in the center of your life will do this. He will direct you down the right path in your relationships, work ethics and how you lead people. Having a "new attitude" is not a new concept. We do it every year on New Year's Day. One of these years, I will see my New Year's resolution through to the end. But think of the feeling that you get with the new set of goals. Think of how focused you are during this time period. That is how you need to approach having God centered in your life. It needs constant awareness to keep the focus and not let it die off like your resolutions do.

A few weeks ago I went golfing for the first time this year. For the past few years I have been too busy to golf and to be quite honest, I am not that good of a golfer. I am average at best but love to play in "scramble" format tournaments. They are the ones where you play the best ball out of the four that your team hits for each shot. That way I do not have to play all of my shots. I started out this day scared that I was going to look like a fool. I was playing a regular game where I was forced to play my ball, good or bad. I had to count all of my shots, including penalty strokes. After six holes, I had already lost three balls and was 15 shots over par. I was frustrated and my attitude was going down hill with every shot. I wondered to myself if I should have even wasted the money on this round of golf. Golf is supposed to be relaxing. This was supposed to be a stress free day. I decided that it was time for a "new attitude". I had been using one type of ball so far and so I figured that "it must be the ball." I would not want to personally take any of the blame for hitting a poor shot, one after another.

I approached the next hole with my "new attitude" and my new brand of golf ball. I was confident (sort of) that things were going to change. A straight drive down the fairway followed. I was close to the 150 yard marker. I stepped up to the ball and confidently hit it onto the green. Wow, I thought. This ball really works. The fact that I held my head down through the whole shot probably paid a bigger part than the ball. I walked up to the green and hit my first putt to within a foot of the hole. I tapped in for par. Now I really had some confidence in this new ball. The next hole was a short par five that I birdied. That is a rarity in my game. I managed to salvage a score of 51 on the front nine. More importantly, I was still using the same ball. I grabbed a burger and a bottle of water and took off for hole #10. I played the back nine holes with confidence. I hit the green on a par three over a pond. That never happens. I was seven feet from the hole and made my putt for a birdie. This is getting exciting now. I finished the second half of the round with a score of 42. This was the best nine holes of my life. Plus, most importantly, I never lost that ball.

I know that it was not the brand of golf ball that changed my game around. It was my attitude. The ball was just the new focus. I was concentrating on the new ball so much that I kept me head down when swinging. I concentrated on my motions more in every shot. I did not take careless risks. Putting God in the center of your life will change your focus. He will keep you down the fairway and out of trouble. You have to make a conscious effort though. It does not come easy at the start. There are too many distractions in life. Too many sand traps and out of bounds areas that we have to look out for. Put Him in the center and you will be truly blessed. What He does for you will show through in what you do for others. Go and try out your "new attitude."

Chapter Five
Creating a Stress Free Work Environment

Let us explore the cause and effect of a stressful work environment. Where does it all begin and can it be avoided. How does your stress affect your team?

You need to start with self evaluation. Are you a stressful person? How does it make you feel? How does it make those around you feel? What does the Bible say about stress?

> Matthew 11:28 (NASB)
>
> Come to Me, all who are weary and heavy-laden, and I will give you rest.

If I'm having a particularly stressful day, I lift up a prayer to God. I know that He will guide me through it. I'm not going through this situation alone. I put my faith in Him, that He will take control of the situation.

He will get me through it. I take a good hard look at what is stressing me. Normally it is a very small think in the overall aspect of life. It is not as big of a deal as we make it out to be. During the moment, it seems so important. When I say that quick prayer, I immediately see my stress level start to go away.

Now we must make it personal. When you start to get stressed, how does it make you feel? Think about your most stressful moment at work recently. I will give you a minute. Think of how it made you feel. What was going through your mind? What were the physical attributes that were going on? How did it affect your work performance? Did you get totally consumed by it? I know what happens to me. I start to get forgetful. I make mistakes or miss other areas that I need to focus on because I get too absorbed in the main item that is stressing me.

But then most important, was it self absorbed, or did you share the moment? Do you know what I mean by sharing the moment? I mean, did you hold those feelings inside yourself or did they shine out of you like a little light and affect everybody around you? You know the situation. It is when you ruin somebody else's perfectly good day with your bad attitude. When you get so overwhelmed with your stress level that arrives off on others around you and they become stressed. Let me describe one of my stressful moments.

I remember catering for about a hundred twenty people in downtown Nashville. It was a summer afternoon. I had a couple of people working with me. We brought in all our supplies. We were catering on the plaza in front of one of the high-rise office buildings. We were aiming for an 11:00 serving time and got there in plenty of time. I do not like to get stressed out over being late so do not wait until last minute to get someplace. Are you the type of person that has your daily commute time down to the minute? You know exactly when you have to leave your house so you can clock in right at the time to start work. You have that meeting with a client across town and you know that it will take twenty minutes to get their but you don't leave the office until twenty minutes before your appointment. That is not me. Trust me, I have many faults. Timeliness, though, is normally not one of them.

As I was working to get the line set up. I had one of my coworkers go to the truck for the food and supplies. He tried to make as few trips as possible. He was trying to be very efficient. This is normally a good trait. I noticed what looked like an attempt to maximize the amount of stuff he could put on the cart. He hit the curb a little bit more force than I guess he thought that he was hitting it to get up onto the sidewalk. Let me point out, that at the top of this cart, was a five gallon igloo dispenser filled with hot cheese sauce. It was an easy way to carry it. It keeps it nice and hot and prevents it from running all over the place. Guess what hit the ground? It was the five gallons of melted cheese sauce. It went all over the edge of the sidewalk and just into the street. To add to the suspense, was that the spilled cheese sauce was about 15ft. away from the valet parking of a major hotel. It is one of the nicest hotels in Nashville. Do you think I was stressed?

I believe that most stress can be eliminated or at least reduced. Think about your daily routine. Do you see a trend day to day? How is your day scheduled? There are some people that start with a daily to do list. No particular priorities or time frames. There are others that are very structured and everything has a time next to it. There are good and bad points about either approach. If you get too structured in your times and do not allow enough downtime in between appointments, you will quickly fall behind on your day. That turns into stress. It starts with when you leave your house to go to work. You have the type of job that requires you to be a work at a specific point in time each morning? Are your hours flexible?

I get into the office around 6:00 am. I do not have to be there that early. Our office opens at 7:30 am. I do not have to worry or stress about rush hour traffic. I can get a lot of work done in that first hour and a half before everyone else shows up. My day starts out very relaxing. I talk to others that describe their experience coming to work as a living hell. Coming in from the southeastern part of town during rush hour traffic is a nightmare. It is slow at best on a good day. Throw in a storm or an accident and you will never make it to work on time if you try to cut it short. If you're the type that tries to sleep in as long as possible and then rush to work, you better not live on that side of town. I have a friend of mine that always complains about the "soccer moms" that are always in his way around the schools during his daily commuting. If you start your day on the wrong note, what makes you think that it is all of a sudden going to be smooth and stress free? Let's try starting out with a heaping serving of stress and wash it down with a strong cup of coffee. That should do the trick. The extra caffeine on top of your stress will make it go away. Not. Make a commitment to yourself to eliminate this part of your stressful day. Leave home early and not have to worry about whether or not you will make it work on time.

As you work throughout the day, think about what causes you stress. I had a manager that worked for me that would get worked up over the smallest thing. Many of these things, she had no control over. I can not count the number of times that I would emphasize the thought of not stressing over what you can not control. Many times it was not work related. Sometimes it was. I would tell her to visualize a box. She needed to put those thoughts that were getting in her way into that box. Now close the box. If it is something personal, try to not open the box until after work. Thinking about it all day long is not going to change anything. So why to let it ruin your day? Channel your energy into what you can control.

It may be the solution or alternative plan that is needed due to a crisis that someone or something caused. Do not dwell in the past. What has happened has happened. It can not be changed no matter how much energy you put into it. So why do we do it? It is because we put our blinders on and are so focused on an exact plan that we do not ever consider that the plan may need to be altered. I had a manager working for me that always wanted a very structured day. If anything got out of timing, they would stress over it so much that it would mess up another part of their day. You have to adapt to change. Things are going to happen throughout the day that are not in your control. You have to accept this. Think about what you want to accomplish throughout the day. Make adjustments when necessary.

What are your plans for lunch? Is it a working lunch or a relaxing lunch? Can it be both? Do not eat at your desk and continue working? You may think that you are gaining ground on the task at hand. This is not so. You are now unfocused and also not allowing your body to relax. I suggest going to the break room where your staff are eating and sit down with them. Have a relaxing conversation with them over lunch. Take the time to get to know them on a personal level. This can show that you care about them. You are part of their team, not just their boss that comes around to critique. OK, I struggle with this one. I eat way too many lunches at my desk. I start to get better for a while. It's easy, though, to slip back into your bad habits. A bag of chips from the vending machine and a bottle of water do not make a good lunch. Sometimes I will tell a receptionist that I'm going out to get some sanity. I might find some lunch along way. It is especially so in the days that I start to get stressed. I feel it coming on. It is the type of day that everybody needs your help. I know that on those days if I had lunch in the break room, they would find me there. It is always "when you have a minute, I could use your help." I know that they do not want to wait 30 minutes for me to finish my lunch to take care of their needs. They're the same people that will walk into my office and expect me to drop the project that I'm working on to take care of their project. By me going out to lunch, it prevents me from being put into the situation. I can take 30 minutes to take time off of work. I notice a big difference when I walk back into the office. It is like I'm starting fresh again.

Philippians 4:6-7 (New Living Translation)

[6] Don't worry about anything; instead, pray about everything. Tell God what you need, and thank him for all he has done. [7] Then you will experience God's peace, which exceeds anything we can understand. His peace will guard your hearts and minds as you live in Christ Jesus.

As your stress builds up, do you know your warning signs that you need to take seriously? Now let us take a look at some signs of stress. Sometimes it will make you feel anxious, irritable or depressed. Do you notice some of that in your own behavior or have you noticed that in some of your co-workers behavior? You might also experience apathy or lack of interest. I know I experience fatigue. But just because I am tired does not mean I am able to sleep. Sometimes that stress level also makes it where you have trouble sleeping at night.

You may experience muscle tension or headaches. Do any of you use alcohol or drugs to cope with stress? Does it really help your stress level? I experience stomach problems from stress. All of us have our signs that our bodies tell us that we are stressed.

If you ignore these warning signs, you will end up with bigger problems. It affects your work performance and ultimately leads to further, more damaging, health problems. You have to listen to your body. There are things that you can incorporate into your day that will reduce your stress.

GET ACTIVE AND MOVING

Aerobic exercise and working up a sweat is an effective way to treat anxiety, increase your energy and relax your body and mind.

This tends to be one of my downfalls, I'll admit it. I tend to not get as active as I need to be. I know that when I have gotten into a routine of going to the gym each morning, then I feel so much better. I have more energy throughout the day. It also relaxes my mind by taking away some of the problems of the day that I would normally be thinking about.

It does not have to be working out at the gym each day. It could be just getting up from your desk periodically throughout the day and go out for a walk. I enjoy taking a walk through the neighborhood in the evenings to clear my mind.

PROPER EATING IS IMPORTANT

Eat small and frequent meals. This helps keep your blood sugar in check. Low blood sugar will make you feel anxious and irritable. Eating too much can make you feel lethargic. This is been another of my struggles over the years. I would start to get stressed, and rush throughout the day. Instead of sitting down for a nice meal that is healthy, I would go through the drive through of the fast food joint and eat all sorts of junk. It is hard to eat salad when driving down the road; it is too easy to me to eat a burger and fries or other fried items. I saw this affect me in multiple ways. Not only did not eat right, I never took time out of my day to just relax.

GET ENOUGH SLEEP

Too little sleep makes you anxious and can hinder your ability to handle stress. When you get stressed, you then have a hard time sleeping. It becomes a vicious circle.

I remember working for an area supervisor that always caused a stressful situation for the managers. I remember going to a managers' meeting where we were talking about staffing levels. The managers had said that they did not have time to go out and recruit staff because they were working too many hours already. I remember working between 80 to 100 hours per week at this time. The area supervisor's response was "Do you sleep at night?" Our response was that we got four to six hours of sleep a night. His response was "don't". I kept waiting for him to show any sign at all that he was kidding, but it never happened

It is possible to get enough sleep a night on a regular basis. You just need to make it a priority. My kids used to give me a hard time when I would come in during the summer from playing outside with them to go to bed by 9:00 at night. But I knew that if I were getting up at 5:00 in the morning that I needed to go to bed at nine to get enough sleep.

DRINK IN MODERATION AND AVOID NICOTINE

Alcohol may temporarily reduce anxiety, but in excess, when it wears off, your anxiety will increase. Not to mention the potential of alcohol abuse. Smoking cigarettes may calm you when you when you are stressed, but nicotine is a powerful stimulant. This just adds to your anxiety level in the long run.

Use time management as your friend when reducing stress. Create a balanced schedule. All work and no play lead to stress. You need to balance your work, family and social life. Don't over commit. You have to learn how to say no. Decide what is a "must" and what is a "should". Prioritize what must be done to accomplish the goal. I find myself involved in multiple organizations and wanting to do it all. This year, I needed to step down from an advisory board for one of these organizations. I felt my stress level rising and felt that I was not doing them justice.

Have you heard someone say that they strive on stress? That is when they do their best work. It is when they are under pressure. They may get a lot of work done. They may push themselves harder to reach new levels of the amount of work that they do. If that is the best work that they can do, then they are falling short of their potential. I can guarantee that their team can do more if they do not have the pressures and stress on them that this person is probably generating.

What makes people feel that they are so strong under stress? Maybe it is that they have never experienced a powerful stress free environment. I remember having our sales director call me up and ask if he could bring a potential client over to one of my cafeterias that I supervised to showcase what we could do for their company. I knew that day that the manager of the cafeteria that he wanted to go to was out sick. I could have called the team and warned them that potential clients were coming. I could hear the staff now. "What do we need to do? Stephanie is out sick. Do we need to change up the menu? What time are they coming?"

I knew that she had empowered her employees to take care of business. They took enough pride and ownership in the account on a regular basis that it was almost running on autopilot. I did not tell them that I was coming over. The client was impressed that everything was going so smoothly during the lunch rush with no one in charge. Actually, they did not see that everyone was in charge. We sold the client on our business and signed a deal for another cafeteria that day.

Let's get back to the cheese sauce incident. You are saying to yourself, "this could cause a lot of stress." I would take the approach that I am only going to stress over what I can control and not what is not under my control. At this point in time there was nothing that I could do to make the cheese sauce disappear from that street. I had to give up control of that particular situation. But I was not about to lose control over my vision. Remember, my vision was to give a great catering experience to my clients.

I immediately picked up the phone and contacted one of my managers at the nearest kitchen to where we were catering. I explained to her that I would talk to her later about what had happened but what I needed her to do now was to start boiling water and prepare more cheese sauce. I had to tell her that there was no time to talk about it. I was pushing the limits as far as time to get the catering ready and that if the water was not already on the burner heating up, she needed to take care of that first.

I then turned to the employee that spilled the cheese sauce and said that he needed to quickly try to scoop up off the ground as much as he could and put in a container and put it on the truck. Do not worry about cleaning it up all the way, just get the bulk of it off the ground and come finish helping to set up the serving line. I took control of the situation at hand and did not let it control me.

The manager showed up, with five minutes to spare, with more cheese sauce that we put on the line. The client never knew what we went through to pull off the catering. Now I know if that you're wondering what happened to the cheese sauce. I glanced over during the middle of the catering and back to the street. I saw the valet attendants with buckets of water washing the cheese sauce down the street. I think back of the priorities that I had. I've talked about the "must do" and the "should do" items. The "must do" is that I needed to have an exceptional catering experience for my clients. The "should do", in this case, is keep that street clean and not spill cheese sauce everywhere.

I have had some teams that have really impressed me with the amount of effort that they put forward and the quality of their work.

I worked the charcoal grill on more occasions than not when doing company catering. Many people would look at me and wonder why I was working that position instead of just supervising and/or making someone else do the cooking.

I knew how much food I wanted cooked and how much I wanted prepared at given times throughout the serving period. Not only did this control the food cost, but it also controlled the food quality.

Now the truth…..I am not good at decorating tables. I am horrible at decorating a serving line. I can give the team a vision of the theme of an event. I can give them a description of the "feel" of the décor and then let them run with it. A co-worker, Stephanie Keller was excellent at taking care of this part of the catering event.

I knew that I was ultimately responsible for the whole event. I did not need to boss people around throughout the event. I gave them ownership and set the vision. They did not have to stress over how much food the people were going to eat or if it were going to be prepared on time.

They were the front line to the customer. They got to experience the excitement and joy of great customer service. I could stay in the background and let them take full credit. It was truly a team effort. They could stay focused on their areas of expertise.

> Proverbs 12:25 (NIV)
>
> Anxiety weighs down the heart, but a kind word cheers it up.

At times, you will see your staff becoming stressed over different situations. As the Bible reads, what you say to them during these stressful times will go a long way toward relieving the stress.

I put one of my most experienced managers on the grill on occasion. It was not a pretty sight. No, I did not say that she did not prepare great food. The stress level on her that radiated into her team was not something that you would brag about.

It got everyone out of their comfort zone. A key to stress management of your team is to know their strengths and weaknesses. You can develop weaknesses into strengths, but ultimately building a strong team is like playing a game of chess. You win the game by having your players in the right spots based on their abilities. You will only be able to do that if you get to know your team. Talk to them and get their opinions. Observe their strengths and weaknesses.

Too often as managers, we believe that we have all of the answers. We have done this so long that no one can tell us how to do it better. It may be a new product we are rolling out or a new line of business opening up. Our ego gets in the way and we forget to ask our employees for their opinions. They are seeing things through another perspective. In some cases as a cashier, they may be seeing it from the customers' perspective because of the feed back that they are getting. Imagine opening a new restaurant and greeting everyone at the front door when they are walking in. You introduce yourself as the new owner or manager. Everyone is excited about the new place and how it looks. They give you all sorts of compliments. Now imagine that you never speak to them again to see what they thought after eating there. Your impression of opening day is that everyone loved it. You are excited about how well your business will thrive.

What happens if most of them did not have a positive experience? How would you know without talking to them when they left the restaurant? What about all of them that would just smile and say that everything was good? You would still have that "looking through rose colored glasses" feeling about your level of accomplishment. You get your true impression of how you did by asking your staff. They were the ones working with the customers. They were the ones that saw the positives and the negatives of the operation throughout the shift. Your team spoke with the customer as a server or cashier and could tell you if the customer liked the food, prices, etc. Tap into the knowledge that they have. Do not go at it alone. This is not the way to improve your team's performance.

A while back, we had somebody doing a new hire orientation, and a salesperson was taking them around the building and introducing them to the staff.

They knew most of the staff that worked there. They got to my office and knew my background. I have worked in a number of departments over the years. I have developed a lot of knowledge over the fifteen years of being in the company. I am somewhat the "go to" person in the office when somebody has a question and they do not know who to ask for the answer. They come to me because at some point time I have probably done that or worked in that area.

They were having a hard time describing my role within the company. They asked me to let the new person know what my responsibilities were. I thought about it for a little bit and I remembered that some staff members for a while called me "Charlie". He is the person in the TV ads for Farm Bureau Insurance that had all the answers. After I thought about it for a minute longer, this is how I responded to their question.

Picture a hurricane. Look at it straight down from the sky. Describe what you see. There is a lot of activity swirling around and in the middle, the eye of the hurricane; there is a sense of calmness. This is peacefulness. Now picture that as being my office and my role. There are so many things going on in the business world right now and there are so many things that you have to try and get done with fewer and fewer people. There has to be something in the center that is pulling it together to keep control of the situation and push forward. That is how I envisioned myself. I am right in the center. There are so many tasks that the managers have to complete each day and many of them involve my input at some time or another. I see the stress of all of their projects that they are juggling throughout the day. Keep your stress outside my office. When you come into my office I want you to stop for a moment and catch your breath. Talk me through what you need and I will provide it so that you can accomplish your goals. When you come into my office and when you are part of my team, I want us to be like a hurricane. I want to be a powerful force to be reckoned with, but under control. I want us to have calmness in the center of the organization.

Chapter Six
Getting the Best Out of Your Team

Why do people go to work each day? Is it for the paycheck or because they love what they do? Do they feel part of a team? Are they proud of what they accomplish each day? I have participated in many surveys over the years asking employees what makes them come back to work each day.

We have asked them "Why do you stay at a job for many years?" "What are your priorities in a job?" Many managers feel that they can not keep good staff unless they raise the budget and give them more money. Good leaders know that money is not the biggest driving factor in job satisfaction. The employee needs to be recognized for a job well done. Employees need to feel that they are respected. They realize that not everything in life and at work is going to be in their favor. They're not going to like every situation that comes up. They just want to be treated fairly. It needs to be fair in their eyes. On the surface it seems pretty easy. The outcome of your decisions may not seem fair to them because they're on the losing end. It is important that they feel that the way that you came up with the decision was fair.

You need to realize that members of your team talk to each other. When you are implementing counseling sessions for improper behavior, you need to be consistent. They do not want to feel singled out. They can accept getting a written warning for something that they know they should not have done if they realize that someone else doing the same thing would see the same results.

Recognize and thank your employees on a regular basis. If they are not doing anything to warrant recognition, you need to look at yourself as their leader. What are you doing to prevent them from being successful? Take personal ownership in their development. Do you give them the tools to be successful? Do they have everything that they need to do the job? Have you taken the time to ask them? How many times do we give up on them before they really get started? You obviously hired them because of their potential. Did they all of a sudden become useless? Look at the training program that you offered them. Was it adequate? When we get busy, we tend to just hire someone and throw them into a position without the proper training. We need someone to do the full job from the beginning. There is no time to wait. What ends up happening is that the employee gets frustrated with the workload that they are not trained to handle. We get frustrated with their performance and we, not knowingly, drive them out of the company. Then we have to interview, hire and train their replacement. This is very costly and time consuming. If we would slow down and train them right, we could probably save quite a few of those frustrated employees that leave. Do not look at their job through your eyes. Look at it through theirs. Ask them what they need. Do they feel that they are getting the proper training? If it is a more experienced employee, solicit their input to the way that the job is handled. They are the ones that do it every day. They are the ones that probably know a more efficient way to do it. Give them the ownership of the process. It never ceases to amaze me the amount of ideas that my team gives me that I never thought of. I will never hear any of it if I think that "I already know it all."

You need to realize that all of your team members have individual talents. If we were all alike, then we would not have balance in our society. Look at the various careers that are available to choose from. We need people to fill all of those needs. Imagine all of the parts of your body and the different roles that each part takes on each day. It takes all of them to have our bodies running smoothly. The same is with your team. It takes all of the different talents to make it work.

> Exodus 35:31-34 (Good News Translation)
>
> God has filled him with his power[a] and given him skill, ability, and understanding for every kind of artistic work,[32] for planning skillful designs and working them in gold, silver, and bronze;[33] for cutting jewels to be set; for carving wood; and for every other kind of artistic work.[34] The Lord has given to him and to Oholiab son of Ahisamach, from the tribe of Dan, the ability to teach their crafts to others.

God gives us all our unique talents. We all have gifts that we need to use each day. As a leader, you recognize what these talents are within your team. You will utilize the talents of each individual for the growth of the team.

I remember working a store in the early 80s and talking with one of my order takers. She was so upset in the fact that the restroom in the facility was always dirty and she did not like using it. We discussed what caused it to get that way and I asked her for her suggestions on how to make it better. She said that no one took ownership of it. No one felt like it was their responsibility. It would slowly get dirty and then no one would care and it would progressively get worse. Finally, I would have to step in and force someone to clean it. She said that she would volunteer to be the one that would clean it going forward if I would support her in enforcing the attitude of keeping it clean with the rest of the staff.

I asked her what cleaning supplies that she wanted to have at her disposal and went out and purchased them. I informed the crew that she was in charge of the restroom and I did not want them to be disrespectful and get it filthy ever again. From that point on, we had the cleanest restroom in town and she took pride in the fact that it was kept up that way.

It would have been real easy for me to just ignore her concerns and continue to let the rest room lack the attention that it needed. I could have just ordered someone to clean it each shift. This may have worked temporarily, but it would have gone back to the way it was after time. By giving her ownership in the process, she took control of the situation and solved the problem. She held her head high in the fact that she was in charge of the rest room. Having that pride at work makes all the difference in the world. It has nothing to do with the type of position or the amount of pay that they receive for it. They need to walk with their head held high. Let them shine.

I have worked with managers that were always worried that if they trained their assistant manager too well, they would take over their position. If someone who was working for them was better than they were, they felt intimidated and would hold them back. They would always be wondering if that person was going to get their job. Without even realizing it at times, they would never give them the praise that they deserved. You need to develop your staff to be better than yourself. If you have team members that are all better than you are and you are the one coordinating their efforts, it just makes you look even stronger. Do not be so paranoid that your team can not get the recognition that they deserve. Be proud of them if they are promoted from your team. It should be a reflection on the way that your team is run as well as their individual talents.

While they are succeeding, it increases the performance of your whole staff. In turn, you indirectly get recognition for what your team achieves. I am honored when I lose one of my staff for a promotion. It makes me feel proud of their accomplishments. I want the other departments and divisions to look to my staff for future leaders. It means that I am successful. If I train my replacement, then it makes my supervisor more confident in promoting me. It is called succession planning. I see this in associations that I have worked with. The board of directors needs to be recruiting and training their successors or they will feel obligated to stay in their position for extra terms that they were not counting on. If the president can groom their vice president to be better than they are, it makes for a smooth transition for the new board.

With the economy going south, everyone has to look at how we can get more work out of fewer people. We need to make sure that we do not go overboard. If you are looking at getting maximum performance out of everyone every minute of every day, you are driving people into burnout. We all know what happens when you burn out your team. You have people that start looking for other jobs. If you have strong team members that you have burnt out, they will easily find another job. I like getting on the line with my staff and challenging them to step up their game. I have a very competitive personality. I am always setting goals for myself and my team that I would do anything possible to obtain.

When challenging my team, I may be able to produce at a faster rate than them and want them to get up to that level. I may be quite slower than them and I want them to be proud of what they do. They can see that they are much stronger and get a chuckle about my struggles at times. They push even harder to surpass my limits even further. This indirectly raises their overall productivity. I also realize that they can not work at that pace all the time. Think of a marathon runner. They do not sprint for the full 26 miles. They keep a controlled pace and pick it up off and on through out the race. They may save enough energy to sprint at the end. They can win the race without being the fastest at all times. Consider this with your team. They do not need to be producing at their highest level 100% of the time. As their supervisor, you get time to relax off and on throughout the day. I am not suggesting they loaf on the job. I just want you to be realistic in their abilities for the long run and not just in the short term.

In the 80s, I was working for Domino's Pizza and they were in their major growth period of the company.

When I started with them, they had about 250 locations. They had over 7000 when I left the company. The way you got ahead as a manager was to prove yourself in your current store and get promoted to a higher volume store. At the time, the managers got a share of the profit as a bonus each month so there was definitely an incentive to grow the business. One of my promotions was to a store that was not doing well due to poor management. They were short staffed and worn out. The manager had not had a day off in about a month. He was burnt out. Remember, this was back when you got your order for free if the pizzas were not delivered within 30 minutes.

Let us think back about the chapter on creating a stress free work environment. This was not it. I was asked by my new supervisor what I would do to "fix" the operation. I told him that I would develop a strong team even if it meant to fire the whole staff and start fresh. Remember, I was very aggressive at the time. Looking back, I could see my style of leadership developing. There were no applicants coming in and I needed staff, including an assistant manager to help me cover all of the shifts.

Everywhere that I went to shop, eat, etc., I would

recruit my staff. We ran short handed for about a month. On the busy nights, we knew that we could not keep up with the amount of business coming in. As we finished the order with the customer, we would explain that it would take approximately 45 minutes to deliver their order and that it would be free. I had set the vision of the store where all employees knew that we were not overly concerned about the short term profits, but were building a client base for the long term. I wanted to give exceptional service in spite of the circumstances.

One particularly busy Friday night, I remember hearing the order taker tell the customer about the delay and that it would be free. She did not stop there. She proceeded to "up-sell" drinks to go with the order. She asked them if they would like to add any sodas to the order and they would be free as well. What a concept! Now you are thinking that this is the craziest thing in the world, but I thought that it was brilliant. Look at it from the eyes of the customer. What were their thoughts when they were honestly told about the delay, promised that there would be no charge as our apology, and then be offered something extra for no apparent reason and no cost as well? Would you be a repeat customer of a restaurant that treated you that way?

After about a month, we were no longer giving away pizzas because we were fully staffed with strong employees that bonded as a team towards the common vision. We doubled the sales within three months and never looked back. I ended up training two assistant managers to the point that they were promoted to their own stores from this location. We were then operating under a stress free work environment. I did not put pressure on them for delivering pizzas late. That was not part of the vision. The vision was to give great customer service (even if there was a cost) so that the customers would become loyal to us.

This empowerment of the employees to do what it takes to reach that goal is what inspired my order taker to do what she did that busy Friday night.

The leader needs to do the long range planning for a company. This is especially true the higher up that you are in management with a company. The Bible shows us about the importance of leading for the long range plan.

> **Exodus 32:34 (New Century Version)**
>
> So now, go. Lead the people where I have told you, and my angel will lead you...

The leader needs to plan out projects carefully. Do not just jump right into things without first considering the costs involved. These may be the costs, dollar wise, of a project. They also may be the longer range costs to the team in the form of strength and morale.

> **Luke 14:28 (New Living Translation)**
>
> But don't begin until you count the cost. For who would begin construction of a building without first calculating the cost to see if there is enough money to finish it

Chapter Seven
Reward, Recognition and Respect

When questioned, most people would not say that they are driven at work to do better due to monetary reasons. Most of what affects them and motivates them fall under these three categories. Reward, recognition and respect are the main areas.

REWARD

When thinking about how to reward your employees, think outside the box. It does not have to be monetary bonuses. Treat them to lunch now and then. For less than $10.00, you can say thank you, I appreciate what you do for our company. Give them a thank you card for going the extra mile. A hand written note from member of management goes a long way. How many employees do you know that would say that they were thanked too much? I have not found the first one. A friend of mine that runs a catering business decided on a hectic day of business to treat her staff. They normally only get the basic sodas for their breaks. This time, however, she went out and purchased a variety of energy drinks and specialty teas. The crew thought that this was an excellent way to say thank you. She probably got an extra amount of energy from her staff because of it as well.

Consider treating a team member and their spouse to a dinner out at a nice restaurant. Showing the spouse that you are appreciative of what they do every day goes a long way. Give the person a day off with pay. You were probably going to pay them anyway, so there is no additional expense. I had a district manager that would come into my cafeteria on Thursday and tell me that he was thankful for all of the extra efforts that I had put in toward catering events and that he was prepared to run my account on Friday. He told me to take a three day weekend and I would still get paid for Friday. It did not cost him any extra money. He did not have to try to justify it when trying to make budget. It just took some extra effort on his part. I personally loved the extra unexpected time off. It showed me that he noticed my efforts. How many times do we notice our employees' efforts but do not acknowledge them. If they feel that we do not notice it looks like we do not care.

Tie your rewards to results. Did they reach a new

milestone? Did they do a special project, or go above and beyond the normal expectations? You do not want it to look like you are playing favorites with your staff. This will do more harm than good. If you are fair, it will make an impact. Bottom line is to remember those two secret words that we do not use often enough, "Thank you!"

RECOGNITION

Give your employees the recognition that they deserve. Honor them in front of their peers. Most wives would rather get flowers delivered to them at work than for you to just bring them home to them. It makes them feel special in front of their coworkers. This same approach works for your staff. Brag about what they are doing in public. It does wonders for self esteem. Once again, it does not have to cost a lot of money if any. Be creative in your thinking. Be highly visible, consistent and fair to your approach to recognition. You want to be honest and sincere.

As a leader, I am always looking for long-term results from my team. When I am interviewing potential candidates to work with me, I look for someone that will be a good fit long term for the company. I did not take the approach that they will be with me forever. I tell them that in my interview with them. I believe that you do not really know a person's potential with your company until you get to know them and their personality. As they work with you, you learn how they work, the way that they think and where their talents are. There are some that tell you that they want to pursue management. I think that part of this is that they want to move up in the company and make more money. People want to grow with a company. This does not mean that everyone wants to get into management. It just means that they do not want a dead end job.

You have to look at the potential of people. Recognize their talents. Figure out how you can use these talents in your organization. It may mean that you give them more responsibility within their department. If there is another opening within the company that you feel that they would be a good fit for, you need to be open to letting them pursue it. If you try to contain them within your team, which is a selfish move, they might find the same kind of opportunity with another company. That is how you lose good talent over time.

You are a career counselor for your staff. If you expect them to be with your company long-term, then you need to meet their career needs. They need to see that they're developing over time. They need to be challenged mentality. It means a lot to them when you can recognize their talents and let them utilize them in a way that it develops them further in their career.

You can apply these principles in all aspects of your life. When my boys were young, they were involved in sports. I helped coach a baseball team that my youngest son, Hunter was on. When I got out to the first practice, I soon realized that we did not have any exceptional talent on the team. The players were average in skill level and I could tell that I had my work cut out for me. The other coach and I were going through different practice drills on the third day of practice trying to see which positions each child would be best suited for. Another boy showed up to practice for the first time that afternoon. I asked him if he had ever played the game before and he responded that he had not. His mom had just bought him a glove and he was there to learn how to play baseball.

We sent him to the outfield and asked him to field some ground balls. The first one hit to him rolled up in front of him and stopped. He picked up the ball in his bare hand and placed it in his gloved hand. At that point, he tried to throw it with his gloved hand. This is where your patience and compassion have to take over. It took extra individual training with this child compared with the rest of the team. We went in to most games knowing as coaches that we would probably lose. We lead the team to believe that their goal was to play their best game, regardless of the outcome of the score. If they played their best, they could hold their heads high when walking off of the field. We did not sugar coat it and tell them that they were all winners no matter what. We taught them the value of having a goal. They learned that it took effort to get good at anything. We taught them that just because they lost the game that it did not mean that they were no good. They were just not the better team that day.

At the end of the game, we had a tradition of giving away the game ball to one of the players. Here was the opportunity for recognition and reward. We could honor a player in front of their peers. We needed to keep the process fair. We would look at the players' performance based on their normal abilities and look for the one that excelled the most. Sometimes it would be a player that hit a home run. They may normally be a good hitter, but today they had an exceptional hit that turned into a home run. Another day, it was the player that normally struck out at the plate that got on base due to a line drive hit into the outfield. These little rewards and recognition went far in developing the boys' confidence in their abilities. By the end of the season, we had beaten some of the top teams in the league. What would have happened if this reward process was not applied fairly?

My oldest son, Kody, played on another team that had the same routine at the end of the game. A player was given the game ball for having an outstanding game. Normally the most talented players got the recognition. Kody is blind in his right eye. This distorts his depth perception to the point that he struggled at the plate and struck out on many occasions. There was one game that he was asked to bunt to get on base each time he got to bat. He successfully got on base every time at bat that game. This was a great achievement for him. The team struggled during that game and lost. The star players did not have good games and the coach was upset with their performance. Two of his sons were the main stars in his mind. When it came time to give away the game ball, he told the players that since they did so poorly, he was not giving it to any of them. This was disheartening for those kids, including Kody, which had good games.

There are opportunities throughout our lives that we

are placed in situations of leadership and can affect the lives of others. I do not want you to get the opinion that only managers at work need to use these guidelines for treating people. We are placed in leadership opportunities all of the time. Too often we just think about how we lead at work.

RESPECT

This is the most important. How does it make you feel when you are respected? You want your team to have that same feeling from you. Doing many of the above suggestions shows your respect. How do you speak to them? What language do you use, both verbal and non-verbal? How many times have you heard executives say that their people are their most valuable company resource? They drive your level of production, quality and customer loyalty.

People do not leave companies. They leave managers. So many managers lack the training, skills or natural talent to become really good managers. They develop the same bad habits of the managers that they work for. I saw that I was going down that road and decided to change my approach. Others never see the flaws in their ways.

Focus on what is good about your staff, not their flaws. If you do not see anything good about them, look at yourself. What are you doing wrong to not be able to get their good qualities to shine through? Do not carry an employee on payroll that disrupts the group due to a poor attitude. If it is because they are just not happy with where they currently are in their career life or they do not enjoy the position that they have, it may be time for a change. If they are not a good fit for your team, then do them a favor and lead them to a better career. It may be in another department with your company or it may be that they need to find another type of position elsewhere that better suits their strengths.

Respect their beliefs, philosophies, personalities and abilities. No two people are the same. If you try to treat everyone exactly the same, you will not get the best out of all of them. People are motivated in different ways. I am not saying to not be fair and consistent. I believe that you need to look at each of them as individuals.

I have worked for managers that cancel vacations for their staff all the time. "Things have changed since I had approved it and I can not let you take the time off" is a typical response when asked why it was cancelled after being approved a couple of months prior. Many times the employee has made plans with their family. What kind of respect does this show for them?

We had just merged with another company in the market. We acquired several members of my staff through the merger of the two company operations. I sat down with each of them to get to know them a little and let them know what to expect out of our company and myself. They were nervous about the change and how it would affect them personally.

One of the questions that I asked all of them was what do they dislike the most out of their current situation with there job. Across the board, they responded that they could hardly ever take vacations since they were the only ones that knew their particular job. I believe that once you commit to scheduling a vacation, you should not cancel no matter what circumstances come up. They deserve their time off and I respect the fact that their vacations are with family members and why should they be punished.

That was easy to promise, but what did I need to do to back it up? I told them all that we were going to cross train everyone in at least one other person's job. It took a while to do this and it seemed at times that they were doing more than what would normally be expected of them. They knew what my vision was, though. They knew that the end result would be uninterrupted vacations when scheduled. Now when someone is out, the others just slide right into their role to fill the gaps.

I now have a much stronger team that is also more respectful of each other. They know what the other goes through everyday. They know that if they cover for a team member's vacation, that person will cover for them. This shows so much respect for one another. Some of them were so used to giving up vacation days that they would see that we were short staffed and ask if they needed to give it up to help the team. I held true to my promise, and made sure that they took the time off. We may fall behind a little on the workload but can make it up later. I feel that if I treat them with respect and do everything in my power to give them time off, they will give me everything in their power while they are on the clock.

Chapter Eight
Respect – The Starting Point

The key to a good relationship is treating people with respect. It starts from the very beginning. You have heard the phrase; "you never get a second first impression." If you start out your relationship with somebody and you are disrespectful to them, you will have a long hard time trying to get that turned around to be able to get a great working relationship. I have heard some say that people have to earn their respect. I disagree. People deserve your respect from day one. Respect comes in many forms. I spoke about listening being one of the important trades have a good leader. Respectful listening means that you listen without interrupting the person that you're talking to. Have you had conversations with people that constantly interrupted you? They are already thinking about their next topic and not paying attention to what you are talking about. They become so self- centered in their conversation and they do not pay attention to the person that they are talking to.

They just want to get to their next subject and do not wait for any feedback.

To be respectful, means to take another person's feelings into consideration. Sometimes it means saying the right things at the right times. Sometimes it means not saying certain things at the wrong time. You can show respect through the spoken word and also through the non-spoken word. Your body language and facial expressions tell a lot about if you care about their feelings. During these conversations you need to keep an open mind. You need to listen to the other person's point of view. You may learn something and change your opinion on the subject.

You need to have honesty and trust in relationships. This applies to both personal and business. Integrity is a serious subject. It goes a long way in showing respect to the people that you work with. You're building a relationship with people. That does not mean that you're always going to agree with them. Some of the most productive conversations that you will have are when you disagree with the person that you're speaking with. It brings out a second perspective to the topic which you are discussing. Keep an open mind. You need to be able to see the other person's point of view. In the end, you may not be able to come to agreement. That is OK. Just remember to be respectful throughout the conversation.

Respect is giving each other space. Sometimes people just need downtime or personal time. Respect this need for them to take some time to heal mentality if that is what they need. We can't always be on the go. Our stress level builds up. We continue to be busy through work and through personal endeavors. You may be able to take a vacation a couple times throughout the year. But what happens during the other fifty weeks. Sometimes you get to a point where you just do not want to deal with people and all. You want to get away. I have come back from vacation many times and have had co-workers ask me what I did for vacation. Did I go anywhere? When I tell them that I just relaxed around the house and did not do anything, they feel that it was a waste of my vacation. These are some of my best vacations. They are the ones that I can really relax. During my last vacation, I spent many hours on this book. There are days that I do not have to do anything. I can sleep as late as I want to. I can just relax and read a book. Some people do not have the ability to just get away from other people and have time to themselves that they need. Sometimes it is time at work that they need to be alone. It is where they have a lot to do and are starting to get stressed in getting it done. Show them respect and just stay away. I have a code system at work based on the amount of work that I have to get accomplished and the time constraints that I am working with. Normally I work with the door wide open. The staff and management can come and go as they please, and they do, and I will drop what I am doing to help them with what is on their mind or the project that they need a report for. The next level is to close the door, but I do not lock it. The blinds on the door are still open so that they can see that I am in there, but obviously busy. They will typically knock and peek in to see if they have permission to come in. The ones that normally would walk right in without asking and their topic of discussion is not that urgent will come back at a later time. If needed, I will lock the door and close the blinds. Some will think that I am out of the office. Some will try the door to see if they can poke their head in and get my attention, find it locked, and wait until later. If it is truly urgent, they knock and I answer the door. If they are truly respectful of my time to get my projects done, in some cases it is payroll and they want to get paid, they would be patient with the door shut and save their projects until later. Think about situations in your own life where people are busy and you interrupt what they are doing to take care of your needs. Was it necessary for the interruption or just your eagerness to take something off of your to do list.

Another way to show respect is to build up somebody's confidence in themselves. We spoke earlier about rewards and recognition. I've never understood why some people felt that it was in their best interest to make somebody else look bad. Is it jealousy on their part that makes them not want to give somebody recognition. A few kind words go a long way. To some people it is a great motivator to give them praise. The praise builds up their own self-confidence which in turn produces better results. Do not just look at someone's outward behavior and assume that they have a lot of self-confidence. I have known people that thrived on being recognized which gave them the confidence to strive for higher levels.

People deserve respect from the very beginning. I believe that if I treat others with respect, it will enable them to treat me with the same respect. That is how I can earn someone's respect. It is a two way street, and it starts with you.

Chapter Nine
It Starts with You

It starts with personal responsibility. You have to take responsibility of your actions. Nobody can dictate how you lead people. Are you a blind follower that never questions the path that you are taking? Stand up and choose the direction of your life. What are your priorities and principles? Are you going to let someone else make those decisions for you? Are you committed to following The Lord's plans for you?

> Proverbs 16:3 (New International Version)
>
> Commit to the LORD whatever you do, and he will establish your plans.

Personal awareness is critical. How do you want to be perceived? Is this how you are currently perceived? Sometimes it is hard to be critical on ourselves. It is difficult to admit our flaws. How do you represent your values and beliefs? I do not mean from your point of view. Look at yourself from the eyes of the people around you. Are you a role model for Jesus?

Do not fall into the corporate trap that says that it is all about results, no matter what the cost. You need to lead by example. We're all supposed to learn from our mistakes. The first step is to admit that you made a mistake. It goes a long way to tell your team that you're sorry. Then learn from your mistake. Your team will be aware this. You are their role model. Think about their perception of you.

> **Romans 12:2 (New Living Translation)**
>
> Don't copy the behavior and customs of this world, but let God transform you into a new person by changing the way you think. Then you will learn to know God's will for you, which is good and pleasing and perfect.

As the Bible tells us, do not get caught up in the way that many managers approach their style of management. I fell into that trap for many years. I was chasing the corporate dream of rising to the top. I mimicked the behaviors of the managers that I worked for. It did not get me very far ahead because it was going against my inner beliefs. It was a constant struggle. I had gone against my own values in life. You can uphold your religious beliefs and still get results. In fact, now I believe that you can get better results because a true leader will always out shine the others in the long run. Your well respected team that has empowerment and ownership in your goals will out produce the competition hands down. They will produce a much higher quality product and your customer loyalty will be second to none. Apply the principles of leadership that are discussed in the Bible and watch as your team grows professionally and personally.

Break the mold. Just because your company culture is one way, does not mean that you have to lead your team that same way. I am not saying that you go against the company goals and vision. You still have objectives that need to be reached. You still need to manage your team and the processes needed to complete the job. The way that you treat your staff needs to show the traits that you have developed as a leader. Do not expect your team to have the same experience if it goes against your value system? Be true to your faith. The expected behaviors are given to us in Scripture. You can still produce the end results required of your team, but through a stronger team approach based on the values and priorities of the biblical ideas presented in this book. My strongest teams over time have been the ones that are led with my spiritual values as the basis.

Think about your own approach. Do you praise more frequently than you criticize? If someone asked your staff, how would they answer the question "Does your supervisor actually care about you?" Perception is reality. You may truly care about them, but does it show in your actions? I challenge you to ask your team to evaluate your performance. I do not mean having them evaluate how much work you produce or the accuracy of your work. Ask them how you're doing as their leader.

- Do I provide to you what you need to do your job?

- Do you feel that you were treated fairly?

- Are my expectations of your performance reasonable?

- What would you like to see me change in regards to the way I lead the team?

- Do you feel that you have my support?

Do not go into this evaluation session with the preconceived notion. This can be a group session with all members of your team present or it could be one on one sessions. I prefer the individual sessions. If they are not opening up to you and giving you honest feedback, then it shows that you do not have the relationship developed that gives them trust in what you will do with the information. If they think that their jobs will be in jeopardy for speaking out, they will have nothing to say. If you can get them to open up with their thoughts, you need to be a good listener. Take a lot of notes. Thank them for their feedback. Most importantly, act on what you just learned.

> **Colossians 3:23 (NIV)**
>
> Whatever you do, work at it with all of your heart, as working for the Lord, not for men.

Temporarily we report to our earthly supervisors. Ultimately we answer only to God. Remember as you do your job, who you are truly working for. It is He that you will answer to in the end. Let His will be done. God may have bigger plans for you. You may not be in the job that He feels will be in your best interest in the long term. I studied accounting and business management in college. I took the path of food service management as my career path. I wanted to lead people and not just work with the financial end of the business. I have always been very analytical and could maximize the profits of my operations because of this. I always wanted to do a job that required both talents.

After awhile, I was resigned to the fact that the accounting side of my career goals was going to dwindle away. God was watching over me, though. Without me even looking for it, a new position in our company was created due to growth that gave me the ability to use my management and accounting skills. I believe that if we follow God's guidance through life, He will always provide for us. Twenty five years after getting out of college, I was doing the line of work that I envisioned when pursuing my degree. It was God watching over me.

Chapter Ten
Stay Grounded in Your Faith

Do you have regular conversations with God? It is crucial to develop your relationship with Him. He is your guiding force. He will give you direction in life if you just listen. God is around us in everything that we do. He is there at all times in our lives. Do you just read scripture or do you study scripture? Do you take the time to see how the words can be looked at from today's perspective? Figure out how to apply it to your daily routine of life.

Get active in your church community. Your relationship with other Christians helps to keep you grounded in your belief system. They help hold you accountable for your actions. That way when you are put into a situation that goes against those beliefs, you are more apt to stand up for what you believe in. You know they would be there to support you in your decisions.

> **1st Corinthians 16:13 (New Living Translation)**
>
> Be on your guard; stand firm in the faith; be men of courage; be strong.
>
> **John 15:5 (New Living Translation)**
>
> Apart from Me, you can do nothing.

I would like to share a story about a leap of faith at my church. On Wednesday evenings, during the school year, we would have a dinner and follow it with small classroom bible studies or small group presentations on religious topics. We had around 100-125 people attend each week during the fall. During the spring, the attendance would fall off due to extra curricular activities of the school kids. We had a staff member coordinating and preparing the meals and there was a set price to offset the expense. After the staff member retired, the church contracted out the preparation of the meals to a local restaurant to cater. The price went up and you were required to make reservations so they knew how much food to bring. After a couple of years of doing this, the attendance dropped to 50-75 people each week. The meal was dropped from the Wednesday night line up for a couple of years.

I mentioned earlier that I do not believe in coincidences. It was early June of 2009 when I was at the church waiting for my son to finish up with hand bell practice. I stopped into Linda's office to chat. We started talking about numerous topics and it came up about my background in food service. Linda helps with the coordination of the Wednesday night education program and the meals. She explained to me that they had a few members of the church that expressed interest in starting up the meal program again. They had a vision of offering a meal that they would have prepared by different teams each week. There would be four team leaders that would get their own volunteers to help them with the meal. This way, they would only be responsible for one meal per month. They envisioned not having a set price and asking for a love offering to offset the expenses. When she asked me if I could help coordinate the meals, I knew that it was God asking me to lead the teams of volunteers. How could I say no to Him?

They needed someone to help with the menu planning, recipes and product ordering. I knew that I could not physically cook the meals due to my work schedule, but all of these tasks could be done behind the scenes. I gladly took on the role. I helped them raise their vision up to another level. We invested in cloth table covers, china plates and silverware. I wanted to give the church members a restaurant quality dining experience and felt that they in turn, would be more generous with their love offerings. We needed to purchase more kitchen supplies since we were anticipating bigger crowds. I empowered these team leaders with the ability to pick a theme each week to coordinate the décor of the room around. They would give me the basics of the menu that they wanted to prepare and I would make suggestions based on what I knew we could handle. These volunteers had never cooked for 200 people before. I needed to give them the tools that they needed to do the job.

There was so much ownership in the new way of catering the meals. Every week, more church members would come to us and ask how they could serve to make this vision come to reality. In fact, it was not unusual to see our pastor helping with the clean up of the dishes at the end of the night. That shows true servant hood. The teamwork that was developed throughout the process was exceptional. It showed through in the preparation of the food, the decorating of the tables and the people walking the room collecting the dishes after the guests were through eating. At the beginning of the second season of this new concept, we topped 300 people in guest counts each week in the fall. These shows how using some of the principles that God has given us, can make a tremendous difference in how a team can operate and the results that can come from it.

We are blessed with opportunities throughout our lives to make an impact. It may be to lead a small project at work. It could be while having a discussion at the dinner table at a Wednesday night meal at church. There are always times that using these principles of leadership help influence the results. Apply the listening techniques to show respect. Empower those around you to help in the creation of your vision. I was talking with a staff member at work and she said that treating people with respect is one of the most important traits that we should have. She has had the discussion with others about whether or not you need to earn someone's respect. I believe that God wants us to treat people respectfully regardless on how they are treating us. It should not matter that we have different ideas or thoughts on a subject. All people should be treated respectfully.

This is one of the principles of leadership that tends to get lost as some corporate managers are trying to get ahead. I was guilty as the next person as I was trying to work my way up the rankings.

Just the other night, a group of us from church went to The Hard Rock Café in Nashville to watch a Sunday school classmate perform a concert. Will Peppers is Christian country music artist. His band performed some of his original songs and some well known favorites from the past couple of decades. It was a very entertaining evening. When his band ended their part of the evening, Will was called back to the stage for an encore. This is where he showed how true he was to his faith. He spoke about his young child and what was truly important in his life. His next song was about just that. Will sang his rendition of the children's hymn "Jesus Loves Me." You do not hear that in a bar on a regular basis. He sang so proudly of his faith. It shows how much he is grounded in that faith. We should be just as proud of our faith in God that it shows through in our jobs.

There are people that ask themselves about the meaning of life. What is their purpose in life? I believe that if you have a strong faith in God, He will guide you through life. He will show you His purpose for you. He has plans for you if you just listen. You can influence many lives of the people that you come into contact with everyday. Apply these guiding principles and you will be amazed and truly blessed with the outcome. When you look back at your life, you will see that you did make a difference.

I saw a saying the other day that read, "I go for a walk and think about my footprints." That spoke to me so much. What kind of an impact am I making with the lives that I touch everyday? I want my faith in Jesus Christ to shine through in everything that I do.

> Galatians 5:22-26 (English Standard Version)
>
> But the fruit of the Spirit is love, joy, peace, patience, kindness, goodness, faithfulness, gentleness, self-control; against such things there is no law. And those who belong to Christ Jesus have crucified the flesh with its passions and desires. If we live by the Spirit, let us also walk by the Spirit. Let us not become conceited, provoking one another, envying one another.

As I was writing this book, I occasionally used voice recognition software. I would dictate different sections and let the computer do the typing. I would read back over what was typed and wonder at times what I had actually said because what came out in print were sentences that just did not make any sense. I do not know if it was because I did not speak slowly enough. It could have been that I did not enunciate my words well enough for the computer to understand. I did notice that whenever I said "God", the computer would type "got." We can relate this principle to our everyday lives. We may think that by our actions and words we are letting God show through. People would be able to see Him in what we do. Too often, this is not the case. We are not clear enough in our words and actions for them to understand what we are saying. We need to be clear enough so that they see what we believe in.

Hold true to your faith and do not be tempted to just blend in with society and the main stream way of managing people. Let God show through in everything that you do. God bless you and keep Him as your guide.

Application in Your Life

> Ezekial 34:12 (English Standard Version)
>
> As a shepherd seeks out his flock when he is among his sheep that have been scattered, so will I seek out my sheep, and I will rescue them from all places where they have been scattered on a day of clouds and thick darkness

How am I entrusted to take care of my team?

_____
_____
_____
_____

> Habakkuk 2:2 (English Standard Version)
>
> And the LORD answered me: "Write the vision; make it plain on tablets, so he may run who reads it.

Do I have a vision and is it well communicated?

_____
_____
_____

Faith Guided Leadership

_____
_____

> Romans 12:8 (NIV)
>
> .... If God has given you leadership ability, take the responsibility seriously. ....

Have a conversation with God. Ask Him what He would like from you in regards to your approach to leadership.

_____
_____
_____
_____
_____

> Luke 2:45-47 (NIV)
>
> 45When they did not find him, they went back to Jerusalem to look for him. 46After three days they found him in the temple courts, sitting among the teachers, listening to them and asking them questions. 47Everyone who heard him was amazed at his understanding and his answers.

Here are my plans to become a better listener.

_____
_____
_____
_____
_____

> Proverbs 15:1 (New Living Translation)
>
> A gentle answer turns away wrath, but a harsh word stirs up anger

Steps I can take to become more responsive to the people that I lead. I will be more aware of how I respond to people.

_____
_____
_____
_____
_____
_____
_____

> **Mark 12:31 (NIV)**
>
> The second is this: 'Love your neighbor as yourself.' There is no commandment greater than these."

How I will focus on respecting others.

_____

_____

_____

_____

_____

> **Colossians 3:12-13 (NIV)**
>
> Therefore, as God's chosen people, holy and dearly loved, clothe yourselves with compassion, kindness, humility, gentleness and patience. Bear with each other and forgive one another if any of you has a grievance against someone. Forgive as the Lord forgave you.

I will be more compassionate toward others by ……………..

_____

_____

_____

_____

_____
_____

> Proverbs 15:21 (English Standard Version)
>
> Folly is a joy to him who lacks sense,
> but a man of understanding walks straight ahead.

How can I be more understanding of others?

_____
_____
_____
_____
_____

> Acts 1:8 (NIV)
>
> But you will receive power when the Holy Spirit comes on you; and you will be my witnesses in Jerusalem, and in all Judea and Samaria, and to the ends of the earth

I can empower my team by doing……

_____

> **Proverbs 12:22 (New Living Translation)**
>
> The LORD hates those who don't keep their word, but he delights and those who do.

Am I a trustworthy person? What is their perception of me?

> **Philippians 4:6-7 (New Living Translation)**
>
> Don't worry about anything; instead, pray about everything. Tell gotten what you need, and thank him for all he has done. If you do this, you will experience God's peace, which is far more wonderful than the human mind can understand. His peace will guard your hearts and minds as you live in Christ Jesus.

> Proverbs 12:25 (NIV)
>
> Anxiety weighs down the heart, but a kind word cheers it up.

How will I reduce my stress level on a regular basis?

_____

_____

_____

_____

_____

> James 5:12 (New King James Version)
>
> But above all, my brethren, do not swear, either by heaven or by earth or with any other oath. But let your "Yes" be "Yes," and *your* "No," "No," lest you fall into judgment.

> Proverbs 11:3 (New Living Translation)
>
> Good people are guided by their honesty; treacherous people are destroyed by their dishonesty.

> Proverbs 20:7 (New Living Translation)
>
> The godly walk with integrity; blessed are their children after them.

What does my integrity say about me?

_____
_____
_____
_____
_____

> Proverbs 11:2 (New Living Translation)
>
> Pride leads to disgrace, but with humility comes wisdom.

Am I humble in the eyes of God?

_____
_____
_____
_____
_____

Psalm 37:7-9 (New Living Translation)

Be still in the presence of the LORD, and wait patiently for him to act. Don't worry about evil people who prosper or fret about their wicked schemes. Stop being angry! Turn from your rage! Do not lose your temper—it only leads to harm. For the wicked will be destroyed, but those who trust in the LORD will possess the land.

What can I do Lord to improve my patience?

_____
_____
_____
_____
_____

Matthew 20:26 (NIV)

"Not so with you. Instead, whoever wants to become great among you must be your servant, and whoever wants to be first must be your slave just as the Son of Man did not come to be served, but to serve, and to give his life as a ransom for many."

> John 21:12-13 (New Living Translation)
>
> "Now come and have some breakfast!" Jesus said. None of the disciples dared to ask him, "Who are you?" They knew it was the Lord. ¹³ Then Jesus served them the bread and the fish.

Lord, I want to be a better servant. Please show me the way.

_____
_____
_____
_____
_____

> Colossians 3:12-13 (New Living Translation)
>
> Since God chose you to be the only people whom he loves, you must clothed yourselves with tenderhearted mercy, kindness, humility, gentleness, and patience. You must make allowances for each other's faults and forgive the person who offends you. Remember the lord forgave you, so you must forgive others.

God, please show me areas of my life that I can be more compassionate with others.

_____
_____
_____
_____
_____
_____

> Matthew 11:28 (NASB)
>
> Come to Me, all who are weary and heavy-laden, and I will give you rest.

Lord, I will lift up my burdens to you. Please comfort me and relieve my stress.

_____
_____
_____
_____
_____
_____

> Philippians 4:6-7 (New Living Translation)

> Don't worry about anything; instead, pray about everything. Tell God what you need, and thank him for all he has done. If you do this, you will experience God's peace, which is far more wonderful than the human mind can understand. His peace will guard your hearts and minds as you live in Christ Jesus.

I will lift up my prayers to you daily. Please help me in these areas of my life.

_____

_____

_____

_____

_____

> Proverbs 12:25 (NIV)
>
> Anxiety weighs down the heart, but a kind word cheers it up.

How can I relieve the anxieties of my coworkers?

_____

_____

_____

_____

> **Exodus 35:31-34 (Good News Translation)**
>
> God has filled him with his power[a] and given him skill, ability, and understanding for every kind of artistic work, [32] for planning skillful designs and working them in gold, silver, and bronze; [33] for cutting jewels to be set; for carving wood; and for every other kind of artistic work. [34] The Lord has given to him and to Oholiab son of Ahisamach, from the tribe of Dan, the ability to teach their crafts to others.

What are some of the talents of my team that I have not noticed and utilized?

Faith Guided Leadership

> Exodus 32:34 (New Century Version)
>
> So now, go. Lead the people where I have told you, and my angel will lead you…

My long term plans for my team are……..

_____
_____
_____
_____
_____

> Luke 14:28 (New Living Translation)
>
> But don't begin until you count the cost. For who would begin construction of a building without first calculating the cost to see if there is enough money to finish it?

I will consider all costs when approaching a new project. Not just the dollar cost.

_____
_____
_____
_____

Notes about:

Reward..........................

Recognition....................

Respect..........................

Faith Guided Leadership

_____

_____

_____

> **Proverbs 16:3 (NIV)**
>
> Commit to the LORD whatever you do, and he will establish your plans.

> **Romans 12:2 (New Living Translation)**
>
> Don't copy the behavior and customs of this world, but let God transform you into a new person by changing the way you think. Then you will learn to know God's will for you, which is good and pleasing and perfect.

> **Colossians 3:23 (NIV)**
>
> Whatever you do, work at it with all of your heart, as working for the Lord, not for men.

My commitments for the future....................

_____

_____

> **1st Corinthians 16:13 (New Living Translation)**
>
> Be on your guard; stand firm in the faith; be men of courage; be strong.

> **John 15:5 (New Living Translation)**
>
> Apart from Me, you can do nothing.

I will pray to God that He will be my guide through life. He will keep me on the path in everything that I do.

> ## Galatians 5:22-26 (English Standard Version)
>
> But the fruit of the Spirit is love, joy, peace, patience, kindness, goodness, faithfulness, gentleness, self-control; against such things there is no law. And those who belong to Christ Jesus have crucified the flesh with its passions and desires. If we live by the Spirit, let us also walk by the Spirit. Let us not become conceited, provoking one another, envying one another.

God, I am committing my life to live by the fruits of the Spirit.

_____

_____

_____

_____

_____

_____

_____

References

MANAGING OR LEADING

1. Ezekial 34:12 (English Standard Version) The Holy Bible, English Standard Version Copyright © 2001 by Crossway Bibles, a division of Good News Publishers.
2. Habakkuk 2:2 (English Standard Version) The Holy Bible, English Standard Version Copyright © 2001 by Crossway Bibles, a division of Good News Publishers.

QUALITIES OF A STRONG LEADER

1. Romans 12:8 (New Living Translation) Holy Bible. New Living Translation copyright© 1996, 2004, 2007 by Tyndale House Foundation.

2. Luke 2:45-47 (New International Version) Copyright © 1973, 1978, 1984, 2011 by Biblica

3. Proverbs 15:1 (New Living Translation) Holy Bible. New Living Translation copyright© 1996, 2004, 2007 by Tyndale House Foundation.

4. Mark 12:31 (New International Version) Copyright © 1973, 1978, 1984, 2011 by Biblica

5. Colossians 3:12-13 (New International Version) Copyright © 1973, 1978, 1984, 2011 by Biblica

6. Proverbs 15:21 (English Standard Version) The Holy Bible, English Standard Version Copyright © 2001 by Crossway Bibles, a division of Good News Publishers.

7. Acts 1:8 (New International Version) Copyright © 1973, 1978, 1984, 2011 by Biblica

8. Donald J. Vlcek, Jr. and Jeffrey P. Davidson, *The Domino Effect* (Copyright © Donald J Vlcek, Jr. 1992

9. Proverbs 12:22 (New Living Translation) Holy Bible. New Living Translation copyright© 1996, 2004, 2007 by Tyndale House Foundation.

WHAT DEFINES YOUR LEADERSHIP STYLE?

1. Merriam Webster Dictionary, http://www.merriam-webster.com/dictionary/personality, accessed July 16, 2011.
2. Myers-Briggs Type Indicator©   researched through https:www.myersbriggs.org accessed July 27, 2011.

3. James 5:12 (New King James Version) Copyright © 1982 by Thomas Nelson, Inc.

4. Proverb 11:3 and Proverbs 20:7 (New Living Translation) Holy Bible. New Living Translation copyright© 1996, 2004, 2007 by Tyndale House Foundation

HOW DOES HAVING GOD IN THE CENTER OF YOUR LIFE INFLUENCE YOUR STYLE?

1. Proverbs 11:2 (New Living Translation) Holy Bible. New Living Translation copyright© 1996, 2004, 2007 by Tyndale House Foundation

2. Psalm 37:7-9 (New Living Translation) Holy Bible. New Living Translation copyright© 1996, 2004, 2007 by Tyndale House Foundation

3. Matthew 20:26 (New International Version) Copyright © 1973, 1978, 1984, 2011 by Biblica

4. John 21:12-13 (New Living Translation) Holy Bible. New Living Translation copyright© 1996, 2004, 2007 by Tyndale House Foundation

5. Colossians 3:12-13 (New Living Translation) Holy Bible. New Living Translation copyright© 1996, 2004, 2007 by Tyndale House Foundation

CREATING A STRESS FREE WORK ENVIRONMENT

1. Matthew 11:28 (New American Standard Bible) Copyright © 1960, 1962, 1963, 1968, 1971, 1972, 1973, 1975, 1977, 1995 by The Lockman Foundation

2. Phillipians 4:6-7 (New Living Translation) Holy Bible. New Living Translation copyright© 1996, 2004,

2007 by Tyndale House Foundation

3. Proverbs 12:25 (New International Version) Copyright © 1973, 1978, 1984, 2011 by Biblica

GETTING THE BEST OUT OF YOUR TEAM

1. Exodus 35:31-34 (Good News Translation) Copyright © 1992 by American Bible Society

2. Exodus 32:34 (New Century Version) The Holy Bible, New Century Version®. Copyright © 2005 by Thomas Nelson, Inc.

3. Luke 14:28 (New Living Translation) Holy Bible. New Living Translation copyright© 1996, 2004, 2007 by Tyndale House Foundation

IT STARTS WITH YOU

1. Proverbs 16:3 (New International Version) Copyright © 1973, 1978, 1984, 2011 by Biblica

2. Romans 12:2 (New Living Translation) Holy Bible. New Living Translation copyright© 1996, 2004, 2007 by Tyndale House Foundation

3. Colossians 3:23 (New International Version) Copyright © 1973, 1978, 1984, 2011 by Biblica

STAY GROUNDED IN YOUR FAITH

1. 1ST Corinthians 13:16 (New Living Translation) Holy Bible. New Living Translation copyright© 1996, 2004, 2007 by Tyndale House Foundation

2. John 15:5 (New Living Translation) Holy Bible. New Living Translation copyright© 1996, 2004, 2007 by Tyndale House Foundation

3. "Jesus Loves Me", written by Anna B. Warner, published 1860.

4. Gallatians 5:22-26 (English Standard Version) The Holy Bible, English Standard Version Copyright © 2001 by Crossway Bibles, a division of Good News Publishers.

ABOUT THE AUTHOR

Tom Mayberry is blessed with a marriage of 23 years to his wife, Cindy. His two sons, Kody and Hunter, are in college and at the age where they are exploring their independence.

Tom has lead teams for over 30 years. He has witnessed the effects of different leadership styles. Throughout his career, his religious faith has grown, and along with it came a refined leadership style. He gives God the glory for what has transpired in his life. It has taken the ups and downs of everyday life to learn what was truly important. His religious beliefs now dictate the way he leads people in business and everyday life.